分子調理の日本食

Molecular Cooking
in Japanese Cuisine

石川 伸一
ISHIKAWA Shin-ichi

石川 繭子
ISHIKAWA Mayuko

桑原 明
KUWABARA Akari

O'REILLY®
オライリー・ジャパン Make:

目次

Table of Contents

まえがき

この本は、仮想の料理本です。載っているレシピは、今のところ、家庭では簡単に作れない"ファンタジー料理"ばかりです。日常のなかで、この料理を作っているキッチンが世界のどこかにあると想像して、ページを眺めてみてください。もしかしたら、近い未来、この本に載っている料理はどの家でも気軽に作れるようになっているかもしれません。

「分子調理」という言葉を聞いたことがあるでしょうか。分子調理は、「分子調理学」と「分子調理法」からなります。分子調理学は、食材の性質の解明、調理中に起こる変化の解明、おいしい料理の要因の解明などを分子レベルで行う"科学"です。それに対して、分子調理法は、おいしい食材の開発、新たな調理方法の開発、おいしい料理の開発を分子レベルの原理に基づいて行う"技術"です。

私たちは、この分子調理法を使い、自分たちに身近な料理を変換することにしました。慣れ親しんだ料理を変えてみることで、使った手法の"能力"が見えやすくなります。

この本の最大の目的は、料理を通して新しい方法とアイデアを試してみることです。メニューには、日本食のなかでも、日常的に食べられるものを取りあげました。各レシピには分子調理学の簡単な解説を加えています。

皆さんは新しい調理法を身につけたとき、自分がこれまで食べてきた料理をどう作り変えるでしょうか?

Introduction

This is a book about fictional recipes. Most of the dishes are "fantasy dishes" that are quite difficult to cook in an ordinary kitchen; however, imagine a "what-if" kitchen somewhere in the world where these dishes can be made. Soon, you may be able to make these dishes in your kitchen.

The field of molecular cooking consists of "molecular cooking science" and "molecular cooking technology." Molecular cooking science is a scientific approach that elucidates food properties, changes that occur during cooking, and the factors that make delicious dishes at the molecular level. "Molecular cooking technology" is a technological approach that develops delicious ingredients, new cooking techniques, and delicious dishes based on molecular level principles.

In this book, we transform Japanese daily meals with molecular cooking techniques. We thought it would be an excellent way to clarify the real capabilities of techniques that have changed things around us.

However, what we wanted to do most was to identify possibilities by trying as many new methods and ideas through cooking that we could conceive. Many of the dishes that are the source of the recipes in this book are typical Japanese family dishes. Each recipe has a brief explanation in terms of molecular cooking science.

You will encounter a new cooking technique one day. How would you accept it, and how would you use it to make new dishes?

ゲル化を調理の過程で上手く使いこなせれば、料理により多様性をもたせることができる。ゲルは、多量の液体を含む固体の状態のものを指す。ゲルがみずみずしさとさまざまな形状を保っていられるのは、ゲル化剤の高分子物質がゲル内で複雑な網目状構造をとっているからである。

1
ゲル化
Gelation

If gelation is appropriately applied to cooking, culinary art will develop and become more diverse. A gel is a solid that contains a large amount of liquid. The gelling agent, as a polymer, forms a complex network structure, retains high moisture content, and holds shape.

分子調理の日本食 | Molecular Cooking in Japanese Cuisine

(Recipe _ 01)

スノードームふろふき大根

Snow globe of simmered daikon radish

透きとおった球体の中で、大根おろしの雪が
降り、ふろふき大根の雪だるまが立っている。そ
のスノードームを支える土台は練りみそだ。レシピ
に使うのは、ふろふき大根用のシンプルな食材だ
が、ひとつだけ見慣れない材料がある。ゲル化
剤のジェランガムだ。

ゲル化とは、流動性のある液体が高い粘性を
持ち、固体になることをいう。ゼリーやババロアに
使われるゼラチンや、水ようかんや杏仁豆腐に使
われる寒天は、よく知られているゲル化剤だ。ゼ
ラチンは薄い黄色みがかった透明色で、寒天は
すこし白濁している。一方、ジェランガムは食品に
使われるゲル化剤の中でも、特に透明度が高い。

透明なジェランガムゼリーを通してみると、あ
たたかなふろふき大根が神秘的な印象になる。

Inside a crystal-clear sphere with flutter-
ing snow of grated daikon, a simmered daikon
snowman stands. The foundation supporting the
snow globe is miso sauce. The ingredients of our
recipe are simple and basic, but one is unfamiliar.
It is gellan gum, a gelling agent.

Gelation is a reaction that causes a fluid liquid to gain a high viscosity and become solid.
Gelatin, which is used for jelly and bavarois, and
agar, which is used for mizu-yókan (soft sweet
red bean jelly) and annin tofu (almond jelly), are
well-known gelling agents. Gelatin gel is transparent with a light yellow color, and agar gel is
slightly milky white. On the other hand, gellan
gum gel is particularly transparent compared to
other gelling agents used in foods.

The transparent gellan gum globe surrounding the warm snowman gives a mysterious
appearance.

材料

- ・大根 … 500g
- ・みそ … 54g
- ・みりん … 30ml（大さじ2）
- ・酒 … 22.5ml（大さじ1と1/2）
- ・砂糖 … 18g
- ・薄口しょうゆ … 5ml（小さじ1）
- ・乾燥こんぶ … 5g
- ・ジェランガム … 2g
- ・塩 … 1g
- ・ゆずの皮（お好みで）

道具

- ・鍋
- ・小鍋
- ・包丁
- ・まな板
- ・おろし器
- ・おたま
- ・へら
- ・くし
- ・スプーン
- ・球状製氷型

手順

1. 大根を2cm程度の輪切りにし、皮をむく。雪だるま型に成形する。

2. 大根おろしを作る。

3. 小鍋に雪だるま型大根と水を入れ、弱火で20分ゆでる。ゆで汁を捨て、一度大根の表面を軽く洗う。

4. 鍋にこんぶ、薄口しょうゆ、下ゆでした雪だるま型大根を入れ、大根が浸かる水を入れる。弱火で30分煮る。

5. 別の小鍋を用意し、水200mlを入れる。そこへジェランガム、塩、大根おろし2gを加え、ジェランガム溶液を作る。沸騰直前までへらでかき混ぜながら中火で加熱する。沸騰したら弱火にし、保温する。ジェランガムは80℃前後で固まり始めてしまうため、できるだけ高温を維持する。

6. 球状製氷型に、③の雪だるま型大根を逆さ（頭になる方が下向き）に入れ、くしで固定する。

7. ⑥に⑤を注ぎ、蓋をする。ゲル溶液の粗熱が取れるまで、時折型をゆすると、大根おろしが全体に分散して見栄えがよくなる。

8. 冷蔵庫に30分置く。しっかりと冷やしてから、つまようじを抜き、型から球体を取り出す。

9. 練りみそを作る。小鍋にみそ、みりん、酒、砂糖を入れ、弱火にかける。砂糖が溶け、全体に照りが出るまでよく練り混ぜ、アルコールの香りが飛んだら火を止める。火を止める前に、お好みで細かく切ったゆずの皮を入れ、よく混ぜても良い。

10. 皿に⑨の練りみそ約10gを置き、その上に球体のゲルを載せる。

INGREDIENTS

- 500 g daikon (Japanese radish)
- 54 g miso
- 30 ml (2 tablespoons)
  mirin (sweet cooking rice wine)
- 22.5 ml (1&1/2 tablespoons)
  cooking sake
- 18 g sugar
- 5 ml (1 teaspoon) light soy sauce
- 5 g dried kombu (kelp)
- 2 g gellan gum
- 1 g salt
- yuzu peel, as you like

UTENSILS

- pot
- small pot
- kitchen knife
- cutting board
- grater
- ladle
- spatula
- skewer
- spoon
- spherical ice mold

STEPS

1. Cut daikon into 2-cm thick rounds and peel it. Shape them into a snowman form.

2. Grate the daikon.

3. Put the snowman-shaped daikon and water in a small pot and simmer on low heat for 20 minutes. Remove the boiling water and rinse the snowman daikon with water.

4. Place kombu, light soy sauce, and cooked daikon into a pot, and pour just enough water to cover the daikon. Simmer them on low heat for 30 minutes.

5. Prepare the gellan gum solution. Pour 200 ml of water and put the gellan gum, salt, and 2 g of grated daikon into a small pot. Heat it on medium, stirring with a spatula until it is just boiling. Turn down the heat to low and keep it heated, with the temperature as high as possible because gellan gum starts to solidify at around 80°C (176°F).

6. Place the snowman daikon (#3) with the head facing down in a spherical ice mold, and fix it with a skewer.

7. Pour #5 into #6, and cover it with a lid. Occasionally shake the mold gently to disperse the grated daikon until the gel solution cools down.

8. Place it in the refrigerator for 30 minutes. When the gel sets, remove the skewer and take out the snow globe from the mold.

9. Prepare the miso sauce. Put the miso, mirin, cooking sake, and sugar in a small pot and heat on low. Mix well until the sugar dissolves, and the whole mixture becomes glossy. Turn off the heat when the alcohol has evaporated. Before turning off the heat, you can add finely chopped yuzu peel.

10. Serve about 10 g of miso sauce (#9) on a plate, and place the snow globe on it.

7

9

10

解説
Explanation

ジェランガムは、他のゲル化剤と何が違うのか？
What makes gellan gum different from other gelling agents?

できあがった「スノードームふろふき大根」を見てまず思ったことは、ドーム内の大根の雪だるまが、実物よりも巨大に見えるということだ。ジェランガムの透明ゲルが、ルーペの凸レンズのようなはたらきをして、中に閉じ込めたものが拡大された。小さく高価な食材もスノードームゲルに入れれば、"ボリュームアップ"が可能かもしれない。

ジェランガムを使うと透明度の高いゲルを作ることができる。そのため、大根おろしなどの白っぽく、粒が細かい食材でも、ゲル中にうまく分散させて固めれば、スノードームにふわふわと舞う雪のように見せることができる。

ジェランガムでできたゲルは、ゼラチンや寒天と比べると弾力性が大きく、やや硬めの質感を持つ。やわらかく煮たふろふき大根と合わせて食べると、食感のコントラストを楽しめる。ジェランガム自体に味はないため、和風だしの風味をほのかにつけても良い。淡い味の大根とゼリーは、練りみそをつけて食べることでより満足感が得られる。

食品添加物として使われるゲル化剤には、ゼラチン、寒天、ジェランガムのほか、ペクチン、カラギーナン、グ
アーガム、ローカストビーンガムなどがある。いずれのゲル化剤を食品に用いた場合でも、長い鎖状の分子が三次元の複雑な網目状構造を取り、この網目状構造の隙間に液体が保持されることで、食品は保水性を持つ。それぞれのゲル化剤によって、ゲル特性やゲル化条件は異なる。ゼラチン、寒天、ジェランガムの性質の違いを表1に示す。

ジェランガムは、水草から採取された微生物が産生する粘質物質である。少量でも非常に強いゲル化力を持つ。また、ゼラチンと違い耐酸性であることから、柑橘類などの強い酸性の果汁が入ったゼリーを作るのにも適している。しかもカルシウムイオン存在下では、熱不可逆性のはたらきで、再加熱しても溶けないゲルになることから、できた果汁入りゼリーは加熱殺菌ができる。

料理のおいしさには、味や香りとともに、食感が大きく影響している。それぞれ特有の性質をもったゲル化剤を適切に使用することにより、目的に応じたさまざまな食感の料理をデザインすることができる。また、複数のゲル化剤を組み合わせて使うことで、これまで味わったことのない食感の料理を創作することも可能である。

The first thing we noticed about this snow globe simmered daikon radish is that the daikon snowman in the globe looks bigger than it is. The transparent gel ball made from gellan gum acts as a convex lens that enlarges the object inside. Even if the expensive ingredients are small, making them appear larger using this trick may be possible.

As gellan gum gel has high transparency, it is possible to create the scene of snow falling by dispersing the grated daikon in the snow globe.

Gellan gum gel is more elastic and slightly more rigid than gelatin or agar. The firm gellan gum gel and the gently simmered daikon have two contrasting textures. As gellan gum itself has no taste, flavoring it with Japanese dashi is recommended. Miso sauce is often used with subtle flavor ingredients in traditional Japanese dishes. This final touch enriches the dish.

Gelling agents used as food additives are gelatin, agar, and gellan gum were already mentioned and also include pectin, carrageenan, guar gum, and locust bean gum. These long chains of molecules form a complex three-dimensional network structure. The network of molecules keeps the liquid in its gaps so that the foods can retain moisture. Each gelling agent has different gelation properties and conditions. The differences in the properties of gelatin, agar, and gellan gum are shown in Table 1.

Gellan gum is a viscous substance produced by microorganisms derived from aquatic plants.

It has a strong gelation ability even with a small amount used in a solution. Since it is resistant to acidity, unlike gelatin, it is suitable for making fruit jellies containing strongly acidic liquids, such as citrus fruit juice. Furthermore, in the presence of calcium ions, the gellan gum gel is thermally irreversible, so it does not melt when reheated. Fruit jellies with gellan gum can be heat-sterilized.

A dish's flavor is important, but texture also has a strong influence on the dish's deliciousness. Utilizing each gelling agent's unique properties makes it possible to design a texture that matches the desirable dish. Furthermore, combining various gelling agents should allow us to create a texture that has never been experienced before.

表1. ゼラチン、寒天、ジェランガムの性質の比較
Table 1. Comparison of gelatin, agar, and gellan gum

	ゼラチン Gelatin	寒天 Agar	ジェランガム Gellan gum
原料 Material	動物の骨や皮（おもに、牛、豚、魚） Animal bone or skin (mainly cows, pigs, and fish)	海藻（てんぐさ、おごのりなど） Red algae (tengusa or ogonori in Japanese)	微生物（Pseudomonas elodea）が産生する粘質物質 Viscous substances produced by microorganisms (Pseudomonas elodea)
主成分 Main component	コラーゲンなどのタンパク質やそれらが分解したペプチド Proteins e.g collagen and the peptides which they break down	多糖類（ガラクトースとその誘導体が細長く鎖状に並んだもの） Polysaccharides (galactose and its derivative bound in an elongated chain)	多糖類（グルコース、グルクロン酸、ラムノースを構成糖とする高分子物質） Polysaccharides (high polymer of constituent sugar e.g. glucose, glucuronic acid, rhamnose)
色・透明度 Color/transparency	透明感のある薄い黄色 Transparent weak yellow	白濁 Milky white	透明 Transparent
融解温度 Melting temperature	40-50℃ (104-122°F)	90-100℃ (194-212°F)	80-90℃ (176-194°F)
凝固（ゲル化）温度 Coagulation (gelation) temperature	10℃以下 Below 10℃ (50°F)	30〜45℃ 30-45℃ (86-113°F)	60〜70℃（カルシウムイオンの存在下では70〜80℃） 60-70℃ (140-158°F) [with calcium ion at 70-80℃ (158-176°F)]
口当たり Texture	やわらかく、独特の弾力を持つ Bouncy, jiggly	粘りがなく、歯切れが良い Not sticky, distinctive firmness	寒天に似るが、より弾力がある Similar to agar, but more elastic
保水性 Water holding capacity	高い High	低い（離水しやすい） Low (easy to syneresis)	高い High
付着性 Adherability	高い High	低い Low	低い Low
熱可逆性 Thermal reversibility	あり（ゲル化能に変化なし） Yes (remain the same for gelation ability)	あり（ゲル化能低下） Yes (decrease in gelation ability)	なし（凝固後は約200℃まで加熱することが可能） No (possible to heat up to 200℃ after fixing)

分子調理の日本食 | Molecular Cooking in Japanese Cuisine

(Recipe _ 02)

耐熱ゼリー天ぷら

Heat-resistant jelly tempura

ジェランガムの大きな特徴のひとつは、高熱に強いことだ。熱不可逆性という性質のおかげで、一度固まったゼリーは約200℃になっても溶けずに、その食感を保つ。ジェランガムでできたゼリーを天ぷらにすれば、揚げたての衣に包まれた熱々のゼリーを食べることができる。

えびやかぼちゃなど、好みの天ぷらタネを半分だけジェランガムに埋めて固め、それを油でカラッと揚げる。いつもの天ぷらとゼリー天ぷらで構成される"ハーフアンドハーフ"の風味や食感を楽しんでみよう。

One of the major characteristics of gellan gum is its resistance to high heat. The solidified jelly will not melt or change its texture up to 200℃ (392°F) because of the thermally irreversible property. If you make tempura from gellan gum gel, you can have hot jelly wrapped in a freshly fried batter.

Prepare your favorite tempura ingredients such as shrimp and pumpkin. Then, cover half of the ingredients in gellan gum and fried. This method allows you to enjoy a traditional and innovative "half & half" tempura.

材料

- サラダ油…1000ml
- だし汁…500ml
- 小麦粉…150g
  （タネ粉付け用…40g、
  天ぷら衣液用…110g）
- えび…4尾
- かぼちゃ…80g
  （スライス4枚、1/8個相当）
- ししとう…4本
- しいたけ…1個
- なす…1個
- 卵…1個
- ジェランガム…5g

道具

- 包丁
- まな板
- ガラスカップ
- ボウル
- 揚げ物用鍋
- 菜箸
- 網しゃくし
- 油切バット
- キッチンペーパー

手順

1. えびは殻をむき、2尾は尾を残す。背ワタを取り、尾を取った2尾は細かく切っておく。沸騰しているお湯にくぐらせ、火を通す。

2. かぼちゃの半分は天ぷら用に薄くスライスし、もう半分はさいの目状に切っておく。ナスは縦に3等分し、両端はヘタの部分を切り落とさないように、縦に切れ目を入れ、扇状に開く。3等分した真ん中はさいの目状に切っておく。ししとうは、高温で破裂しないように胴体に穴を開ける。しいたけは半分に削ぎ切りにする。それぞれをゆでておく。

3. だし汁を用意する。ジェランガムを添加し、中火で加熱する。いったん沸騰させてから、弱火にする。

4. ガラスカップに①と②を入れた後、③を流し込む。冷蔵庫内で冷やし固める。固まったゲルをカップから取り出す。

5. 天ぷら衣液を作る。ボウルに卵と水150mlを入れ、かき混ぜる。さらに小麦粉110gを加えて混ぜる。

6. ④の全体に小麦粉をまぶしてから、天ぷら衣液にくぐらせる。160℃に熱したサラダ油で揚げる。中の具材およびゲルはすでに加熱済みなので、衣に火が通れば良い。

7. 網しゃくしですくい上げ、キッチンペーパーを引いたバットで油を切る。

8. 皿に盛る。

INGREDIENTS

· 1000 ml salad oil
· 500 ml dashi stock (Japanese soup stock made from fish and kelp)
· 150 g flour (40 g for ingredients, 110 g for batter)
· 4 shrimps
· 80 g (4 slices, 1/8 of a whole) pumpkin
· 4 shishito green peppers
· 1 shiitake mushroom
· 1 eggplant
· 1 egg
· 5 g gellan gum

UTENSILS

· kitchen knife
· cutting board
· glass cup
· bowl
· frying pot
· cooking chopsticks
· skimmer
· tray
· paper towel

STEPS

1. Peel and devein four shrimps, and remove the tails on two of them. Remove the tails of the other two shrimps and dice them. Lightly boil the shrimps.

2. Cut half of pumpkin into thin slices and dice the other half. Slice eggplant into three lengthwise pieces. Remove the top of the center piece and dice it. Make vertical cuts on both sides pieces and open them like a fan shape. Make a hole in the shishito green pepper's body to prevent it from bursting at a high temperature. Cut shiitake mushroom into half. Boil all the vegetables.

3. Put dashi stock and gellan gum in a pot and heat on medium. Turn down the heat after it comes to a boil.

4. Place the shrimps (#1) and vegetables (#2) in glass cups. Pour the dashi and gellan solution (#3) in them. Place the mixture in the refrigerator to set the gel. Take out the shrimp and vegetable jellies from the cups.

5. Prepare the tempura batter. Put the egg and 150 ml of water in a bowl and stir them. Add 110 g of flour to them and mix.

6. Coat the jellies (#4) with flour and dip them into the tempura batter (#5). Fry them in salad oil at 160°C (320°F) until the batter is cooked because the ingredients and gel inside are already heated.

7. Scoop up the tempura with a skimmer and place them on paper towels with a tray to drain off the oil.

8. Serve on a plate.

ジェランガムの分子構造が高温で
溶けないゼリーを作る

The molecular structure of gellan gum creates a jelly
that does not melt at high temperatures.

ゲルだけをタネにして天ぷらにしても全体の味に大きな変化がないため、一般的な天ぷらのタネであるえび、かぼちゃ、なすなどをゲルに半分だけ埋め込み、それに衣をつけて揚げてみた。「通常の天ぷら＋タネ入りゲル天ぷら」という"ハイブリッド天ぷら"である。

完成品は、ゲルのかたまりからえびなどが飛び出す不思議な形の天ぷらであるが、切ってその断面を見てみると、透明なゲルに埋め込まれたタネのようすが美しい。ジェランガムは耐熱性が高いゲルのため、高温の油で揚げても溶けることなく形が保たれている。ゲル天ぷらを切っても離水は見られない。

この天ぷらを食べると、ゲル、衣、ゲル中の具材、ゲル外の具材など、数種類の食感とそれらの変化を楽しむことができる。また、ゲルはそのままでも食べられるため、ゲル中に埋める具材に火を通す必要がなければ、外側の衣に近い部分は熱いゼリー、中心部は冷たいゼリーという温度勾配のある天ぷらもできる。

なぜ、ジェランガムのゲルは油で揚げるといった高温の調理をしても溶けないのか。ゼリーの分子構造に着目すると答えがわかる。ゼラチンも寒天もジェランガムもタンパク質や多糖類の高分子化合物で、ねじれたバネのような構造を持つ。これらを水に混ぜて高温で溶かすと、通常、バネの構造がゆるんで流動性のあるゾルになる。このゾル状態では、分子が伸びたコイルのような構造をしていて、水を抱えきれないため、固体としての形を保つことができない。液体状のゾルを冷やしていくと、分子構造はもとの固いバネの形に戻り、さらにバネ同士がお互いに絡み合って、複雑な網目状構造となる。この網目状構造の中に水が抱え込まれると、全体が固まったゲルになる。

固まったゼラチンと寒天は溶かした時と同程度の温度に加熱することで、再びバネの構造がゆるんで水を抱えきれなくなり、その結果、形を保てなくなるが、ジェランガムは再加熱しても溶けにくく、その構造が維持される。その理由は、カルシウムイオンと結合してできたジェランガムゲルの構造がきわめて安定しているため、熱によって崩されないからである（図1）。

In order to create various tastes and textures in one food, only half of the ingredients (shrimp, pumpkin, and eggplant) were encased in the gel. After dipping it into the batter and frying, a "hybrid tempura" with half of the typical ingredients and half gel ingredients is ready.

The finished tempura has an unfamiliar shape, with the shrimp protruding from the solid gel. When cut and the cross-section is viewed, the ingredients floating in the transparent gel look beautiful. Gellan gum has high heat resistance, so it keeps its shape after frying in oil. Syneresis is not seen in the gel.

With this tempura, you can enjoy the various textures of the gel itself, the tempura batter, and the ingredients individually or with the gel. Additionally, since the gel can be eaten without heating, it is possible to make the tempura at various temperatures. The gel tempura is hot on the outside and cold on the inside because it was made using pre-cooked ingredients.

Why does the gellan gum gel not melt even when cooked at high temperatures, such as frying in oil? The answer is shown by the molecular structure of the jelly. Gelatin, agar, and gellan gum are high polymer compounds of proteins or polysaccharides with a twisted spring-like structure. Dissolving the compound-water mixture at high temperatures causes the structure of the springs to become loosened, and the mixture becomes a fluid sol. The polymers have an elongated coil-like structure in the sol state and cannot keep water or hold the shape like a solid. As the liquid sol cools down, the molecules gradually return to the firm spring structure. Each spring is tangled up, and a complicated net-like structure is generated, and the water is trapped in the net-like structure; the gel is set.

If the solidified gelatin and agar are reheated to the same temperature as when they were melted, they will not retain their shape due to the spring structure loosening again. On the other hand, gellan gum is difficult to melt even when reheated, and the gel shape is maintained because the gellan gum gel's structure, which is formed by binding with calcium ions, is extremely stable and will not be destroyed by heat (Figure 1).

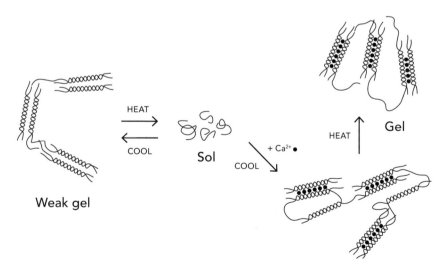

図1. ジェランガムのゲル化のモデル図
Figure 1. Gelation model of gellan gum

分子調理の日本食 | Molecular Cooking in Japanese Cuisine

カレーライス麺

Curry rice noodles

「カレーライス」は学校の給食でも人気があり、多くの人にとって子どものころからなじみ深いメニューだ。明治時代に日本に伝わったカレーは独自の進化をとげ、カレーライスの他にも、カレーうどんやカレーラーメンなど「カレー麺」のメニューが生まれた。

ゲル化剤を使うと、カレーライスをまるごと麺のかたちにすることができる。まず、カレーとご飯をあわせ、ジェランガムを加えたものを細長いチューブの中に入れて固める。その後、チューブから中身を取り出すと、麺状になった「カレーライス麺」の完成だ。

カレーメニューの歴史の中でライスと麺に分類されたものが、今、ゲル化剤の力で合体することになった。

Curry rice is one of the most beloved school lunch items in Japan. It has been familiar to many Japanese people since their childhood. Curry was introduced to Japan at the beginning of the 20th century, and since then, it has been developed in various unique ways. In addition to Japanese-style curry and rice, curry and noodles made with udon or ramen were invented.

Whole curry and rice dishes can be converted into a noodle shape by mixing curry and rice with gellan gum, injecting the mixture into a thin tube, and waiting until they are set. The "curry rice noodle" is complete after taking out the contents from the tube.

What had been categorized into rice and noodles in the history of the curry has now been united into one using gellan gum.

材料

- ・インスタントカレールウ … 80g
- ・炊飯米 … 30g
- ・ジェランガム … 2g
- ・塩 … 2g
- ・福神漬け (お好みで)

道具

- ・小鍋
- ・へら
- ・ざる
- ・おたま
- ・ゴムチューブ (内径3mm、50cm)
- ・注射器
- ・ブレンダー

手順

1. 水750mlにカレールウを入れ、中火で加熱しながらルウを溶かす。沸騰後5分ほど経ったら、火を止める。これをカレースープとする。

2. 別の小鍋でカレースープ100mlと水100mlを混合する。

3. 炊飯米に浸る程度の水を入れ、ブレンダーにかける。米粒の大きさがゴムチューブの直径より小さくなるまでブレンダーで粉砕する。

4. ざるで③の水気を切り、②の鍋に入れる。

5. ジェランガムと食塩を④の鍋に加え、ジェランガムが完全に溶けるまで、よくかき混ぜながら中火で加熱する。沸騰後は弱火にする。焦げ付かないように注意する。これをカレーゲル溶液とする。

6. カレーゲル溶液が熱いうちに注射器で吸い上げ、ゴムチューブに流し込む。

7. 5分ほど常温でチューブを冷やす。冷却後、注射器に水を入れ、カレーゲル溶液と同じようにゴムチューブに流し、ゲル麺を押し出す。

8. 押し出したゲル麺を皿の上に渦巻き状に並べ、福神漬けをお好みで添える。

INGREDIENTS

· 80 g instant curry roux
· 3 g cooked rice
· 2 g gellan gum
· 2 g salt
· fukujin pickles, as you like

UTENSILS

· small pot
· spatula
· colander
· ladle
· rubber tube (id 3 mm, 50 cm)
· syringe
· blender

STEPS

1. Prepare the curry soup. Put the curry roux and 750 ml of water in a small pot and simmer on medium. After 5 minutes, turn off the heat.

2. Put 100 ml of curry soup and 100 ml of water in a pot and mix them.

3. Add enough water to cooked rice and crush the rice grains with a blender until they become smaller than the diameter of the rubber tube.

4. Transfer #3 to a colander and put it in #2.

5. Prepare the curry gel solution. Put gellan gum and salt in #4. Heat on medium, stiring frequently until the gellan gum is completely dissolved. After it comes to a boil, turn down the heat to low.

6. Suck up the curry gel solution with the syringe and inject it into the rubber tube while it is hot.

7. Cool down the rubber tube at room temperature for 5 minutes. Once #7 is cooled, fill the syringe with water and inject it into the rubber tube to push out the gel noodles.

8. Arrange the gel noodles in a spiral on a plate, and serve with fukujin pickles garnish.

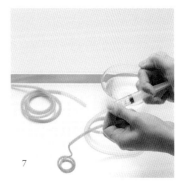

なぜ料理をトランスフォーメーションするのか？
What is the reason for transforming dishes?

　　カレーライス麺は細長い形をしているが、光沢のある不思議な質感を持った"未来っぽい"麺だ。その異質感から、麺の定義について考えさせられてしまう。ちなみに、日本における「麺」は、広義の意味では細長い形状が特徴の食品のことである。カレーライス麺は小麦粉で作った麺のようにグルテンによる弾力性はない。食感は柔らかく、口に入れるとすぐにほろっと崩れる。味はまぎれもなくカレーライスである。

　　麺の中にカレーとご飯を一緒に埋め込むために、ジェランガムを使った。ジェランガムでゲル化することで食感が変わるとともに、料理の風味の強さに変化が生じる。また、食べ物の温度も味や香りに大きく影響する。このレシピではカレーライス麺をチューブから出すのに冷やす必要があるため、麺の香りの分子は通常の温かいカレーより放出されにくく、香りは感じにくい。香り分子が放出されにくい理由には、カレーをゲル状に固めていることもあるだろう。一方、味はゲル化することでカレーの分子が、舌の上に留まりやすくなるためか、塩味などを強く感じやすい。そのため、薄くても十分にカレーの味を感じることができる。減塩食品の満足感を高めるのに、ゲル化剤の利用は良いだろう。

　　このレシピのカレーライス麺を作るのに、内径が3mmのチューブを使った。チューブの形状を変えれば、麺の見た目や食べごたえを自在に変えられる。平たく伸ばして固めれば、カレーライスゲルシートができる。また、ゲルを固める道具の形やゲルの弾力性を工夫することで、マカロニのような筒状のカレーライスもできるかもしれない。

　　高齢化社会における深刻な社会課題のひとつに、誤嚥の問題がある。嚥下機能が低下した人の多くは、誤嚥により食べ物が気管や肺の中まで入ってしまうことで、命に関わる誤嚥性肺炎を引き起こす恐れがある。その解決策として求められているものは嚥下調整食である。この食品の重要な特徴のひとつが、飲み込まれるときにある程度のまとまり（食塊）になっていることだ。また、誤嚥のリスクとなる液体を含んでいないことも重視される。そこで大きな働きをしてくれるのが、ゼラチン、カラギーナン、ジェランガムなどといった保水性の高いゲル化剤である。これらの食材は、ゲルの強度や温度による変化などそれぞれの特徴があるので、添加する料理に合わせてうまく選択すると良いであろう。このカレーライス麺は、未来の嚥下調整食のショーケースである。

Curry rice noodle has a long, thin shape, and its surface has a glossy, strange texture. It may be a futuristic noodle, which prompts to reconsider what it means to be a noodle. Noodles in Japan are foods that have a long and thin shape in a broader sense. The curry rice noodle does not have a chewy texture like gluten noodles made from wheat flour. It has a soft texture and falls apart immediately on the tongue. The taste is obviously that of curry and rice.

Gellan gum was used to combine curry and rice into the noodles. This gelation changes the texture and flavor intensity of the food. The temperature of the food also affects the taste and aroma. As the curry rice noodles need to cool down before removal from the tube, the noodle's aroma molecules are released less than those of typical warm curry. The gelation described above is another reason why the aroma molecules are difficult to release. However, as for the taste, it is easier to perceive the curry rice noodle's saltiness because the gel helps the curry molecules stay on the tongue. Therefore, it gives the curry, even with less salt, a strong taste. That means the gelling agents can be used to increase the satisfaction of low-sodium foods.

In this recipe, the tube with an inner diameter of 3 mm was used for making the noodles. By altering the shape of the tube, the appearance and texture of the noodles can be changed easily. Curry rice gel sheets can be made by flattening and setting the gel. Moreover, by arranging the shape of utensils and adjusting the elasticity of the gel, it may be possible to make tubular-shaped curry rice like macaroni.

One of the serious social subjects in an aging society is the problem of accidental swallowing. Many people whose swallowing function is decreased can accidentally swallow and get food in the trachea and lungs. Therefore, dysphagia diets that are easy to swallow are demanded. One of the necessary conditions of these foods is to form a food bolus when swallowed. Moreover, they need to contain no liquids that have a risk of accidental swallowing. The thickening agents with high water holding capacity like gelatin, carrageenan, and gellan gum work well to solve these problems. Since these ingredients have their properties, such as gel strength or temperature requirements, it would be better to choose an appropriate gel according to the dish. This curry rice noodle is a good showcase of the future of dysphagia diets.

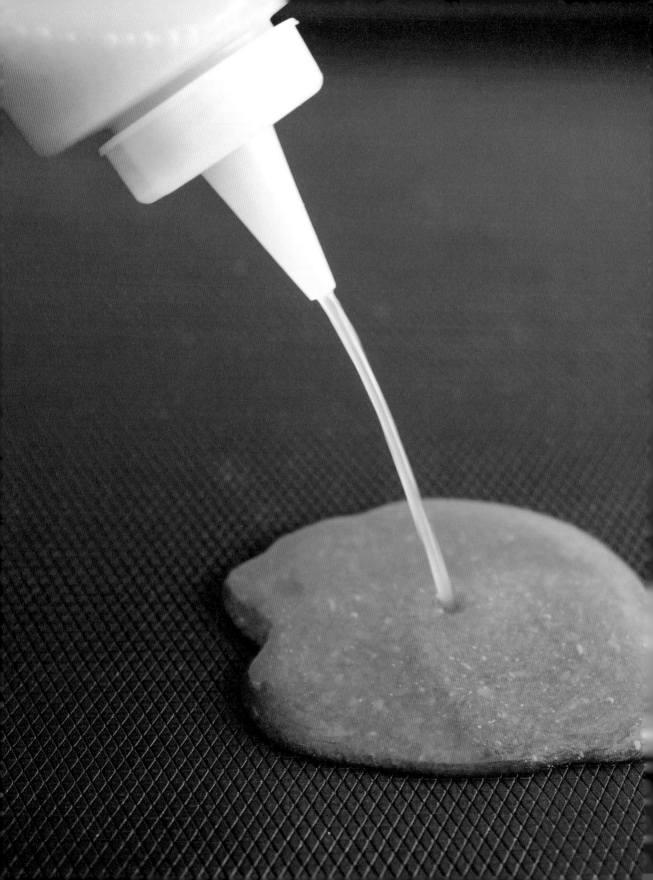

ゲル化剤の中には、加熱によって食材をゲル化させる性質を持つものがある。その作用は熱ゲル化と呼ばれている。熱ゲル化により、熱々のゼリーができたり、ゲルの水分が飛ぶことで食品がシート状になったりする。料理の全体的な構造を大きく変えることができる方法だ。

2

熱 ゲ ル 化

Thermogelation

With some gelling agents, heating causes the foods to gelation. That reaction is called thermogelation. The reaction produces a hot jelly and the removal of water from the jelly results in a sheet of food. The technique can significantly change the overall structure of the dish.

温めると固まり、冷やすと溶けるけんちん汁

Harden on warm and melt on cool, kenchin-jiru soup

お椀の中に汁を盛り忘れたわけではない。この温かな汁物の"汁"は、固体のかたちをしていて、具と一緒にお箸でつまんで食べるのだ。熱々のしょうゆ風味の汁は、プリンのようなぷるぷるとした食感をしている。

液体の汁を固体に変えるために使ったのは、メチルセルロースという食品添加物で、食品加工の現場でも食品の粘度を上げるときなどに利用される。メチルセルロースは高温で固まり、低温で溶ける性質を持つ。

この熱々の固体の"汁"は冷めるにつれて、段々溶けて液体になる。食べ進める時間の経過とともに汁の食感が変わっていく、不思議な一杯だ。

The pouring of the soup into the bowl has not been accidentally forgotten. This warm "soup" has a solid state so that it can be picked up with chopsticks and eaten. This piping hot, soy sauce-flavored soup has a jiggly pudding-like texture.

Methylcellulose, one of the food additives, transforms the liquid soup into a solid form. It is often used to increase the viscosity of foods in the food processing field. Methylcellulose has the property of solidifying at high temperatures and melting in low temperatures.

This hot solid soup gradually becomes liquid as it cools, so the texture of the soup changes with time. It is like a magic soup.

材 料

- だし汁 … 400ml
- 豆腐 … 120g
- 5%メチルセルロース水溶液
        … 100ml
- さといも … 80g
- 大根 … 50g
- にんじん … 20g
- ごぼう … 20g
- 長ねぎ … 20g
- しょうゆ … 15ml（大さじ1）
- 油 … 10ml（小さじ2）
- 酒 … 7.5ml（小さじ1と1/2）

道 具

- 包丁
- まな板
- 鍋
- ざる
- ボウル
- 計量カップ
- シリコン型
- 電子レンジ

手 順

1. 大根、にんじんは3mm厚のいちょう切り、さといもは4〜5mm厚の輪切り、長ねぎは1cmのぶつ切りにする。ごぼうは2mm厚に薄切りし、水にさらしてあく抜きをする。

2. 鍋に油を引き、大根、にんじん、ごぼう、さといもを入れ、軽く炒める。さらに豆腐を加え、崩しながら炒める。

3. ②にだし汁と酒を加え、中火で15分煮る。野菜が柔らかくなったらねぎを加え、ひと煮立ちさせる。

4. しょうゆで味を整えてから冷やす。

5. 冷めた煮汁150mlを計量カップにとり、5%メチルセルロース水溶液を添加し、よく混ぜる。

6. ⑤をシリコン型に注ぐ。

7. 500Wの電子レンジで4分間加熱し、ゲル化させる。型の容量によって加熱時間を調整する。

8. ゲル化した煮汁ゲルをお椀に盛り、その周りに水気を切ったけんちん汁の具材を盛る。

2

4

5

INGREDIENTS

· 400 ml dashi stock
· 120 g tofu
· 100 ml 5% aqueous methylcellulose solution
· 80 g taro
· 50 g daikon
· 20 g carrot
· 20 g burdock
· 20 g green onion
· 15 ml (1 tablespoon) soy sauce
· 10 ml (2 teaspoons) oil
· 7.5 ml (1&1/2 tablespoons) cooking sake

UTENSILS

· kitchen knife
· cutting board
· pot
· colander
· bowl
· measuring cup
· silicon mold
· microwave oven

STEPS

1. Cut daikon and carrot into 3-mm thick quarter-rounds, taro into 4 to 5-mm thick rounds, burdock into 2-mm thick slices, and green onion into 1-cm pieces. Soak the burdock in water to remove the harsh taste.

2. Pour a little oil into a pot, and fry lightly daikon, carrot, burdock, and taro. Add tofu to them and fry it while breaking it up.

3. Add dashi stock and cooking sake to #2 and simmer on medium heat for 5 minutes. When the vegetables are all cooked, add green onion, and bring the soup to a boil.

4. Add soy sauce to the pot and let it cool.

5. Pour 150 ml of the cold soup (#4) into a measuring cup, add 5% methylcellulose solution to it, and mix well.

6. Pour #5 into a silicon mold.

7. Heat #6 in a microwave oven at 500W for 4 minutes to set a gel. Adjust the heating time according to the capacity of the mold.

8. Place the solidified soup gel in a bowl and arrange the vegetables around it.

6

7

8

メチルセルロースの特殊な "ループ" が熱ゲル化をもたらす
A special "loop" of methylcellulose is involved in thermogelation.

　熱い汁が、やわらかい弾力のあるゼリーになっているけんちん汁である。日本料理や中華料理でとろみをつける料理に水溶き片栗粉を用いたあんかけがあるが、あんかけでぷるぷるとした食感を出すのは難しい。一方、ぷるぷるとしたゼラチンのゼリーを温めれば熱で溶けてしまう。この不可能なはずの「ホットゼリー」を可能にしているのが、メチルセルロースである。

　メチルセルロースは変わった性質を持った食品添加物である。ゲル化剤を使った食品は高温になると粘度が低下してやわらかくなり、低温になるほど硬くなるものが多い。しかし、メチルセルロースは反対に、高温で固体になり、低温で液体になるという性質を持っている。このメチルセルロースで作ったゲルは、冷めるとだんだん溶け、再度加熱すればまた固まる。この性質は、「熱ゲル化」と呼ばれている。

　メチルセルロースは、植物の細胞壁の主成分であるセルロースを化学的に変化（化学修飾）させることで作られる。また、メチルセルロース同様、セルロースを原料として化学修飾して作られるものにカルボキシメチルセルロースというものもある（図2-1）。

　これらの高分子は水への溶けやすさが異なる。セルロースは、冷水にも熱水にも溶けない。メチルセルロースは冷水に徐々に溶けるが、熱水には溶けない。カルボキシメチルセルロースは冷水にも、熱水にも溶ける。

　メチルセルロースもカルボキシメチルセルロースも、食品の粘性を上げる食品添加物（増粘剤、安定剤、ゲル化剤）として使われている。メチルセルロースはその水溶液の温度が上がると固まるが、カルボキシメチルセルロースは高温になってもゲル化せず、固まらない。

　海藻に含まれるアガロースやカラギーナンなど、食品に使われるほとんどの多糖類は、水に溶けた状態の場合、基本的には温度が上昇すると粘度は低下する。また、微生物が産生する多糖類のキサンタンガムは温度による粘度の変化は見られない。メチルセルロースの粘度は、温度の上昇によって高くなり、さらに、冷却によってまた元に戻るというループ状の変化を起こす（図2-2）。メチルセルロース水溶液は「ゾル⇄ゲル」という、加熱と冷却を繰り返してももとに戻る「可逆性」を持っている食材である。一方、加熱するともとに戻らない「不可逆性」の食材には卵の卵白などがある。

Kenchin-jiru is a Japanese traditional hot soup made with vegetables in a soy sauce-based soup. The kenchin-jiru in this recipe is the hot soup turned into a soft, bouncy jelly. Potato starch is used to make a thick starchy sauce in Japanese and Chinese cuisines. However, it is difficult to get a jiggly texture with this ingredient. On the other hand, the bouncy gelatin jelly melts if it is warmed up. Methylcellulose makes it possible to have a "hot jelly" that seemed otherwise impossible.

Methylcellulose is a food additive with unusual characteristics. Many foods with gelling agents become softer as the viscosity decreases at high temperatures and become harder at low temperatures. However, the properties of methylcellulose are the opposite. It becomes solid at high temperatures and liquid at low temperatures. The gel made with methylcellulose gradually melts as it is cooled and solidifies again when reheating it. This mechanism is called "thermogelation."

Methylcellulose is made from cellulose, the main component of the cell wall of plants, by chemical modification. Additionally, carboxymethylcellulose is produced by chemically modifying cellulose (Figure 2-1).

These polymers differ in their solubility in water. Cellulose is insoluble in cold and hot water. Methylcellulose is soluble in cold water but insoluble in hot water. Carboxymethylcellulose is soluble in both cold and hot water.

Both methylcellulose and carboxymethylcellulose are used as food additives (thickeners, stabilizers, and gelling agents) that increase the viscosity of foods. Methylcellulose solidifies as the temperature of the water solution increases, while carboxymethylcellulose does not.

Most polysaccharides used in food, such as agarose and carrageenan in seaweed, when dissolved in water, decrease the viscosity as the temperature increases. Furthermore, the viscosity of xanthan gum, one of the polysaccharides produced by microorganisms, is not affected by temperature. The viscosity of methylcellulose changes in a loop such that it increases with temperature and returns to its original state with cooling (Figure 2-2). Methylcellulose solution is an ingredient that undergoes a "sol-gel" reaction, which shows reversibility and returns to its original state even with repeat heating and cooling. On the other hand, egg white is one of the irreversible ingredients that do not return to their original state once heated.

図2-1. セルロース類の構造式
Figure 2-1. Structural formula of cellulose and its derivatives

Cellulose

R=H or CH$_3$
Methylcellulose

R=H or CH$_2$COOH
Carboxymethylcellulose

図2-2. 各種ゲル化剤の温度と粘度の関係図
Figure 2-2. Effect of temperature on the viscosity of gelling agents

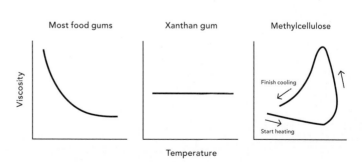

Most food gums

Xanthan gum

Methylcellulose

Viscosity

Finish cooling

Start heating

Temperature

変わりすぎ助六寿司

Origami sukeroku-sushi

助六寿司は、いなり寿司と巻き寿司の折り詰めのことだ。

分子調理法を使うと、助六寿司は折り紙に変身する。

いなり寿司の油揚げとメチルセルロースを混ぜて焼くと、"油揚げの紙"ができあがる。三角に折って寿司飯を包めば、クレープのようなかたちのいなり寿司ができる。巻き寿司の具材は、全部まとめて一枚のシートになる。華やかな色合いのストライプ模様をしたシートは、黄色い部分が卵焼き、ピンク色が桜でんぶ、緑色がきゅうり、茶色がかんぴょうだ。

シート状の寿司ネタは、見た目のように風味もほのかで柔らかくなる。ガリのシートで折った折り鶴を添えて、優しい味をいただく。

Sukeroku-sushi is a sushi set consisting of inari-sushi and sushi rolls.

This sukeroku-sushi is transformed into origami paper by molecular cooking technology.

The mixture of abura-age (inari-sushi ingredient) and methylcellulose is baked into "abura-age paper." You can then fold the paper into a triangle and use it to wrap sushi rice. It becomes a new style of crepe-like inari-sushi. All the sushi ingredients of sushi rolls are combined together into a single sheet. The colors of the traditional ingredients stripe the sheet; yellow is from the tamagoyaki, pink is from the sakura denbu, green is from the cucumber, and brown is from the kanpyo.

The taste of the sheet-shaped sushi ingredients is as soft and mild as it looks. Garnish the plate with an origami crane made from a pickled ginger sheet and enjoy the gentle taste.

材料

- ・寿司飯…350g
- ・5%メチルセルロース水溶液
  …132ml
- ・きゅうり…45g
- ・いなり用味付き油揚げ…40g
- ・ガリ…40g
- ・卵焼き…30g
- ・かんぴょう…30g
- ・桜でんぶ…5g

道具

- ・ボウル
- ・菜箸
- ・スプーン
- ・フライ返し
- ・巻きす
- ・スクイズボトル
- ・ブレンダー
- ・ホットプレート

巻き寿司
Sushi rolls

2

手順

［巻き寿司］

1. 卵焼きに重量の3倍の水を加え、ブレンダーで攪拌する。きゅうり、かんぴょうも同様に準備する。桜でんぶは重量の5倍の水を加え、ブレンダーで攪拌する。

2. 卵焼き、きゅうり、かんぴょうを砕いたものに5%メチルセルロース水溶液22mlを加え、攪拌する。桜でんぶを砕いたものには5%メチルセルロース水溶液6mlを加え、攪拌する。

3. ②をそれぞれスクイズボトルに移し替える。

4. ③をホットプレートの上に広げる。75℃～90℃で1時間加熱し、具材シートを作製する。

5. シートが乾燥したら、端からゆっくりはがす。

6. 巻きすのうえに具材シートをしき、その上に寿司飯をのせる。手前から奥に向かって巻き、形を整え、食べやすい大きさに切る。

［いなり寿司］

1. いなり用味付き油揚げに重量の3倍の水を加え、ブレンダーで攪拌する。5%メチルセルロース水溶液30mlを添加し、さらによく混ぜる。

2. ①をスクイズボトルに移し替え、ホットプレートのうえに正方形に広げる。

3. 75℃～90℃のホットプレートで1時間加熱し、油揚げシートを作製する。乾燥後、端からゆっくりはがす。

4. 油揚げシートを好きな形に折り、寿司飯を詰める。

［ガリ］

1. ガリに重量の3倍の水を加え、ブレンダーで攪拌する。5%メチルセルロース水溶液30mlを添加し、さらにブレンダーで攪拌する。

2. スクイズボトルに移し替え、ホットプレートのうえに正方形に広げる。

3. 75℃～90℃のホットプレートで1時間加熱し、ガリシートを作製する。乾燥後、端からゆっくりはがす。

4. 好きな大きさに切り、折って形を作る。

INGREDIENTS

· 350 g vinegared sushi rice
· 132 ml 5% aqueous
    methylcellulose solution
· 45 g cucumber
· 40 g seasoned abura-age for inari
· 40 g pickled ginger
· 30 g tamagoyaki (Japanese omelet)
· 30 g kanpyo (dried gourd shavings)
· 5 g sakura denbu
    (fluffy sweet fish flakes)

UTENSILS

· bowl
· cooking chopsticks
· spoon
· turner
· rolling mat
· squeeze bottle
· blender
· hot plate

巻き寿司
Sushi rolls

STEPS

Sushi rolls

1. Add three times the weight of water to the tamagoyaki and mix with a blender. Do the same process to cucumber and kanpyo. Add five times the weight of water to the sakura denbu, and mix with the blender.

2. Add 5% methylcellulose solution to each ingredient (#1) and mix individually. Add 22 ml of the solution for the tamagoyaki, cucumber, and kanpyo. Add 6 ml of the solution for the denbu.

3. Transfer #2 to a squeeze bottle separately.

4. Pour and thinly spread #3 on a hot plate to produce a sheet. Heat at 75°C (167°F)–90°C (194°F) for 1 hour.

5. When the sheet dries, carefully peel it from the hot plate.

6. Place the sheet on the sushi mat and spread the vinegared sushi rice across the sheet. Roll them from the front to the back, shape the sushi into a round and slice it.

Inari-sushi

1. Add three times the weight of water to the seasoned abura-age and mix with a blender. Add 30 ml of 5% methylcellulose solution and mix well.

2. Transfer #1 to a squeeze bottle and spread it in a square form on a hot plate.

3. Heat at 75°C (167°F)–90°C (194°F) for 1 hour. When the sheet dries, carefully peel it off.

4. Fold the sheet into a triangle shape and stuff it with sushi rice.

Pickled ginger

1. Add three times the weight of water to the pickled ginger, and mix with a blender. Add 30 ml of 5% methylcellulose solution and mix well.

2. Transfer #1 to a squeeze bottle and spread it in a square form on a hot plate.

3. Heat at 75°C (167°F)–90°C (194°F) for 1 hour. When the sheet dries, carefully peel it off.

4. Fold the sheet into an origami crane.

メチルセルロースの
「温めると固まり、冷やすと溶ける」
メカニズムとは？

What is the mechanism of methylcellulose,
which solidifies on warming and melts on cooling?

巻き寿司の具材であるかんぴょう、卵焼き、きゅうり、桜でんぶといった具材をひとつのシートにして、海苔の代わりに巻くと、かわいい見た目の巻き寿司ができあがる。いなり寿司の油揚げもシート状にすることで、手巻き寿司のように寿司飯を巻くことができる。ガリをシート状にすれば、食べられる折り鶴を作ることもできる。

このようなシートは、通常の助六寿司で使われる具材とメチルセルロースを混ぜ、ホットプレート上にうすく広げ、ゆっくり低温で加熱することによってできあがる。メチルセルロースの熱ゲル化を利用すれば、基本的にはどんな具材でも熱で固めてから水分を飛ばすことで紙のようになる。食材のみで同じような乾燥処理をしても、きれいなシート状になるものは少ない。

シートの食感は、使った具材によって異なる。巻き寿司の具材であるかんぴょうやきゅうりは、しっとりとした食感になるが、卵焼きはやや固い食感になる。食感の違いは、食材の脂質やタンパク質などの成分が影響していると考えられる。メチルセルロースの濃度も食感に影響する。

なぜ、メチルセルロースが「熱ゲル化」、すなわち温めると固まり、冷やすと溶ける性質を持つのか。その理由は、メチルセルロースの分子構造にある。

低温下では、水分子が、メチルセルロース分子のヒドロキシ基 (Hydroxy group, -OH) やメトキシ基 (Methoxy group, CH_3O-) の周りを取り囲み、クラスターが形成され、粘度が低いゾルの状態になっている。温度が約50℃以上になると、メチルセルロースのメトキシ基に結合している水のクラスターが壊され、メトキシ基の疎水基同士で相互作用が生じる(図2-3)。その結果、メチルセルロース分子がしっかりした構造となり、安定したゲルになる。さらに、そのまま加熱するとゲルが脱水されシート状になる。

メチルセルロースの特徴的な性質である熱ゲル化は、メチルセルロース分子の側鎖が温度の違いによって、水分子と結合するか、またはメチルセルロース同士で互いに結合するかという現象が関係している。

Instead of wrapping sushi rice in nori, wrap it in a sheet made from all sushi roll ingredients such as tamagoyaki, cucumber, kanpyo, and denbu. This creates a sushi roll adorable and colorful. By making abura-age into a paper form, you can roll sushi rice with it. The abura-age for inari can also be made into a sheet to roll up sushi rice, like hand-rolled sushi, and the pickled ginger sheet can be used to make edible origami cranes.

The material of the edible sheets is a mixture of usual sukeroku-sushi ingredients and methylcellulose. Spread it thinly on a hot plate and heat it slowly at low temperatures to complete the sheet. By utilizing thermogelation of methylcellulose, nearly any ingredients can be transformed into a paper-like form. Even if the same drying process is performed with only the ingredients, a few of them form a clean sheet.

The texture of these sheets depends on the ingredients. A sheet made with cucumber or kanpyo has a soft texture, while a tamagoyaki sheet has a slightly hard texture. The differences in the texture would be influenced by the fat and protein components of the ingredients. Additionally, the concentration of methylcellulose would affect the texture.

Why does methylcellulose have a property of thermogelation that causes the gel to solidify when heated and melt when cooled? The reason lies in the molecular structure of methylcellulose. At low temperatures, methylcellulose in an aqueous solution is surrounded by clusters of water molecules around the hydroxy (-OH) and methoxy (CH_3O-) groups of its molecule, resulting in a sol state with low viscosity. At temperatures above about 50°C (122°F), the water clusters bound to the methoxy groups of methylcellulose are broken, and the hydrophobic methoxy groups interact with each other (Figure 2-3). As a result, the methylcellulose solution has a solid structure and becomes a stable gel. Furthermore, the gel is dehydrated to form a sheet when it is continuously heated.

Thermogelation, the characteristic property of methylcellulose, is related to the differences in the binding mechanism of methylcellulose molecules depending on the temperature.

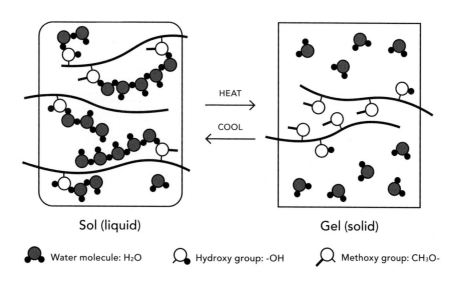

Sol (liquid) Gel (solid)

HEAT
COOL

● Water molecule: H_2O ○ Hydroxy group: -OH ○ Methoxy group: CH_3O-

図2-3. メチルセルロースの熱ゲル化のモデル図
Figure 2-3. Thermogelation model of methylcellulose

逆ロールキャベツ

Reversed cabbage roll

ひき肉をキャベツの葉でくるんで煮込むとロールキャベツができる。ジューシーな肉汁をキャベツで閉じ込めた料理は、おいしさの理屈にかなっている。

一方で、まったく新しいメニューを考えるとき、突拍子もない考え方を試してみるのもいいかもしれない。ひき肉をキャベツで包むのがロールキャベツなら、関係をあべこべにして、キャベツをひき肉で包んだものは、"逆"ロールキャベツということになる。これを、メチルセルロースを使って作ったら、なぜか大輪の花ができてしまった。

皿の上で開いた花の中心はキャベツでできた熱いゼリーのボールで、周りを囲む花びらは肉でできた薄く繊細なシートだ。肉のシートにキャベツのゼリーを巻いてほおばる。

Cabbage roll, simmered wrapping ground meat in cabbage leaves, is one of Japan's home-cooked dishes as in other countries. The juicy meat is trapped in the cabbage, which fits the logic for bringing out the deliciousness.

It might be helpful to try a strange idea to invent a new dish. If the definition of cabbage roll is to wrap ground meat in cabbage, how about making it the other way around and wrapping cabbage in ground meat? That is the reversed cabbage roll. Making the reversed cabbage roll with methylcellulose, surprisingly, produced a big flower on the plate.

The blooming flower center is a ball of hot jelly made from cabbage, and the surrounding petals are thin sheets made from ground meat. Wrap the cabbage jelly with the meat petals and take a bite.

材料

- ・キャベツ…150g（外側3枚程度）
- ・豚ひき肉…100g
- ・5％メチルセルロース水溶液
  　　…85ml
- ・玉ねぎ…50g
- ・卵…30g
- ・油…30ml（大さじ2）
- ・コンソメ顆粒…8g
- ・パン粉…5g
- ・牛乳…5ml（小さじ1）
- ・塩…3g
- ・コショウ…少々

道具

- ・包丁
- ・まな板
- ・フライパン
- ・蓋
- ・木べら
- ・ボウル
- ・計量カップ
- ・フライ返し
- ・スクイズボトル
- ・スプーン
- ・シリコン型
- ・ブレンダー
- ・ホットプレート

手順

1. みじん切りにした玉ねぎを、油を引いたフライパンであめ色になるまで中火で炒める。ボウルに豚ひき肉、卵、パン粉、牛乳、炒めた玉ねぎ、塩、コショウを入れてよくこね、ハンバーグの種を作る。30gずつ4等分し、空気を抜きながら成形する。熱したフライパンに油を引いて、ハンバーグを焼く。

2. ボウルに①のハンバーグ60gをとり、水180mlを加え、ブレンダーで攪拌する。

3. ②に5％メチルセルロース水溶液45mlを添加し、さらにブレンダーで攪拌する。

4. ③をスクイズボトルに移し替え、ホットプレートの上にしずく形に広げたものをいくつか作る

5. 75〜90℃のホットプレートで一時間加熱し、シート肉を作製する。乾燥したら端からゆっくりとはがす。

6. 鍋に水450mlとコンソメ顆粒とキャベツを入れ、中火で加熱する。沸騰してから5分間加熱した後、火からおろし冷ましておく。

7. ⑥から、キャベツ30gと煮汁60mlを取り、ブレンダーで粗く砕く。

8. ⑦に5％メチルセルロース水溶液40mlを加え、さらにブレンダーで攪拌する。

9. シリコン型に⑧を注ぎ、500Wの電子レンジで4分間加熱し、ゲル化させる。型の容量によって加熱時間を調整する。

10. ⑤のハンバーグシートと⑨のキャベツゲルを皿に盛りつける。

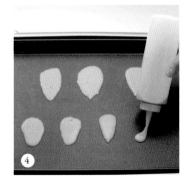

INGREDIENTS

· 150 g (about 3 outer leaves) cabbage
· 100 g ground pork
· 85 ml 5 % aqueous
    methylcellulose solution
· 50 g onion
· 30 g egg
· 30 ml (2 tablespoons) oil
· 8 g consommé granules
· 5 g panko (bread crumbs)
· 5 ml (1 teaspoon) milk
· 3 g salt
· a pinch of pepper

UTENSILS

· kitchen knife
· cutting board
· frying pan
· lid
· pot
· bowl
· measuring cup
· turner
· squeeze bottle
· spoon
· silicon mold
· blender
· hot plate

STEPS

1. Finely chop onion and fry it in an oiled frying pan over medium heat until golden brown. Put ground pork, egg, panko, milk, fried onion, salt, and pepper in a bowl and knead them. Divide them into four equal portions of 30 g each and shape them into patties. Broil them in a frying pan.

2. Put 60 g of #1 in a bowl, add 180 ml of water to it, and mix with a blender.

3. Add 45 ml of 5% methylcellulose solution to #2 and mix it again.

4. Transfer #3 to a squeeze bottle. Pour it into elliptic shapes on a hot plate.

5. Heat at 75℃ (167°F)–90℃ (194°F) for 1 hour. When the sheets dry, carefully peel them off.

6. Put 450 ml of water, consommé granules, and cabbage in a pot and simmer on medium heat for 5 minutes. Turn off the heat and let cool.

7. Take 30 g of the cabbage and 60 ml of the soup from #6 and mix them while crushing the cabbage roughly with a blender.

8. Add 40 ml of 5% methylcellulose solution to #7 and mix it again.

9. Pour #8 into a silicon mold and heat in a microwave oven at 500W for 4 minutes to set a gel. Adjust the heating time according to the capacity of the mold.

10. Arrange the meat sheets (#5) and the cabbage gel (#9) on a plate.

8

9

10

分子調理法で料理の構造を反転できる
Molecular cooking technology can invert the structure of dishes.

　メチルセルロースの「熱ゲル化」と「シート状になる性質」の両方を利用して、ロールキャベツの内側と外側が"逆"になる料理を作った。つまり肉のシートでキャベツのゲルを包む料理である。シートで熱いゲルを包んだ状態にすると、乾燥した肉シートが水分を吸ってどんどん柔らかくなっていくので、さまざまな食感を楽しめるように、キャベツのホットゲルのまわりに肉シートを並べる盛り付けにした。肉シートでキャベツのゲルを巻いたり、シートにゲルを乗せたりして食べる。口の中で感じる風味は、通常のロールキャベツに近いものだ。メチルセルロースそのものには風味がないため、逆ロールキャベツの場合も、基本的に素材の風味が活かされている。

　新しい見た目、風味、食感の料理を創り出そうとするとき、世界中の食材が比較的簡単に入手できるようになっている現在では、新しい食材を見つけて、そのものの風味や食感で勝負することがなかなか難しい。一方で、食材の風味を活かしながら食感だけを変化させることは、逆ロールキャベツのように比較的簡単にできるうえに、大きな驚きをもたらすことができる。風味ではなく食感に新境地を求め、食品添加物を料理に使うことは、その過剰使用に対して批判が生じる場合があるものの、何か新しくておもしろいものをつくろうとする上でのひとつのアプローチだといえる。

　ちなみに、食品衛生法で、メチルセルロースの使用量の上限は食品重量の2％以下とされている。一般的に、業務用の食品添加物として売られている粉末のメチルセルロースは水にすぐ溶けないが、冷蔵庫に入れてゆっくり時間をかけて溶解することで、透明でねっとりとした流動性を持つゾルとなり、調理に使用しやすくなる。

This is the dish in which the inside and outside of the cabbage roll are reversed. Two properties of methylcellulose have been utilized to make that dish. They are thermogelation for the hot cabbage gel and the sheet forming property for the meat sheet. The sheets are placed around the gel instead of wrapping the gel in a sheet because the dry meat sheets soften with the gel moisture. In this presentation, you can wrap the cabbage gel in the meat sheet or put the gel on the sheet for various textures. The flavor of the hot cabbage gel wrapped in the meat sheet is close to the traditional cabbage roll. As methylcellulose itself has no flavor, it is possible to enjoy the flavor of the original ingredients.

When trying to create a dish with a totally new appearance, flavor, and texture, it is difficult to make a novel dish with only ingredients. This is because it has now become easy to get ingredients from all over the world. On the other hand, changing the texture while keeping the flavor of ingredients is easy to try, like reversed cabbage roll, and can bring us a great surprise. Food additives must be used in cooking to seek new frontiers in texture rather than flavor. Sometimes their overuse can be criticized. However, they could be one approach to creating something new and interesting.

Note that the upper concentration of methylcellulose usage required by the Food Sanitation Act in Japan is 2% or less of the food weight. Powdered methylcellulose, which is sold for commercial use as a food additive in general, does not dissolve immediately in water. It becomes a transparent and viscous sol when placed in the refrigerator and slowly dissolved over time, a tip to use methylcellulose more easily.

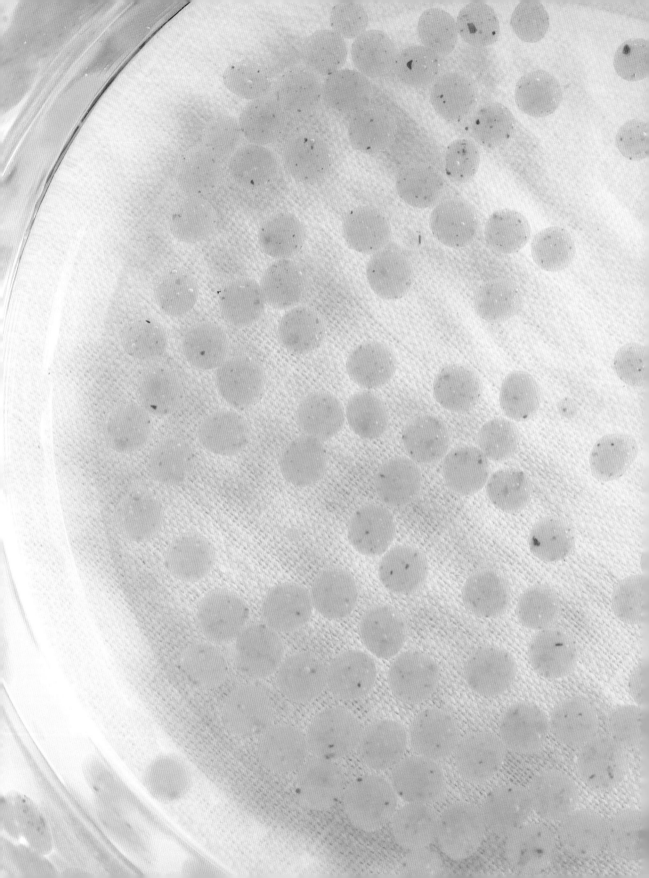

球状化とは、一瞬で薄いゲルの膜が形成され、液体が包み込まれて球の形になることである。その膜は、アルギン酸とカルシウムイオンの化学反応によってできたものだ。球状化は、日本で発明された人工イクラの技術を元に発展し、分子調理法で最も有名な方法の一つになった。

3
球 状 化
Spherification

Spherification is the process in which a thin gel membrane is instantly formed that envelops the liquid, forming a sphere. The chemical reaction of alginic acid and calcium ions produce the membrane. Spherification was developed based on the artificial ikura (salmon roe) technique invented in Japan and has become one of the most famous molecular cooking methods.

　分子調理の日本食 ｜ Molecular Cooking in Japanese Cuisine

水炊きに添える
フレーバーキャビア

Flavor caviar for mizutaki

　水炊きは日本の代表的な鍋料理のひとつだが、今回の料理の主役は、それに添えられたフレーバーキャビアだ。フレーバーキャビアは、薄い膜に包まれた小さな米粒大の球体で、中には調味料の液体が入っている。鍋の具を取り分けた皿に、たくさんの種類のフレーバーキャビアの中から好みの味を選んで、好きなだけふりかけて食べる。数種類を散らして、オリジナルの配合を試すのも楽しい。

　アルギン酸塩入りの調味料の液体を、カルシウム水溶液の中に滴下すると、溶液同士は混ざり合わず、両者の間に膜ができて、アルギン酸塩の水滴は球状になる。この操作は球状化と呼ばれ、代表的な分子調理法のひとつである。

Mizutaki is a typical hot pot dish in Japan, but the leading player in our recipe is the "flavor caviar" on the side of the hot pot. This flavor caviar is a rice-grain-sized sphere of liquid seasoning encased in a thin membrane. Choose your favorite flavor from many kinds of caviar, and sprinkle as much as you like on the hot pot ingredients. It is also fun to customize the types of flavor and make your original combination.

When the liquid seasoning with sodium alginate is dropped into an aqueous calcium lactate solution, the liquids do not mix. A membrane is produced between the liquids, and the water droplets of sodium alginate form a sphere. This process is called spherification. It is one of the leading molecular cooking technology.

材料

・好きな種類の液体調味料 … 100ml
・乳酸カルシウム … 3g
・アルギン酸ナトリウム … 1g

道具

・ボウル
・おたま
・網しゃくし
・スクイズボトル
・ブレンダー

手順

1. 液体調味料100mlに、アルギン酸ナトリウムを添加する。

2. ブレンダーで混ぜる。

3. 大きなボウルに水を100ml入れ、さらに乳酸カルシウムを添加する。乳酸カルシウムの白色沈殿物がなくなるまでよくかき混ぜる。

4. ②をスクイズボトルに移し、③の乳酸カルシウム水溶液に滴下する。

5. 乳酸カルシウム水溶液内で球体を約30秒間静置後、網しゃくしで引き上げ、水で軽く洗う。

INGREDIENTS

· 100 ml liquid seasoning
　　(anything you like)
· 3 g calcium lactate
· 1 g sodium alginate

UTENSILS

· bowl
· ladle
· skimmer
· squeeze bottle
· blender

STEPS

1. Add sodium alginate to 100 ml of liquid seasoning.

2. Mix with a blender.

3. Put 100 ml of water and calcium lactate in a large bowl. Mix well till the white precipitate of calcium lactate dissolves.

4. Transfer #2 to a squeeze bottle and drop it into the calcium lactate aqueous solution (#3).

5. Leave the spheres in the calcium solution for about 30 seconds. Scoop them up with a skimmer and rinse them with water.

1

2

4

5

フレーバーキャビアの薄い膜を形作るものは？
Why does the thin film of flavor caviar form?

　水のみでゆでて、具材からだしを取る水炊きは、素材の風味をじっくり味わうことができるが、食べる時にポン酢しょうゆなどの調味料で風味を足すと、よりおいしい。また、鍋料理では、ねぎ、もみじおろし、柚子胡椒などの薬味を使って、味を変化させながら食べることもよく行われている。

　しょうゆ、みそ、キムチ、ごまだれなどの液体調味料を、イクラのように球状化することで、風味に加えて弾ける食感を水炊きに付与することができる。さらに、しょうゆとキムチのキャビアを合わせることで、しょうゆキムチ風味、みそとごまのキャビアを合わせることで、みそごま風味など、風味を簡単にアレンジすることもできる。3種類のフレーバーキャビアを作れば、その組み合わせは7通り、4種類で15通り、5種類で31通りと、何通りもの組み合わせの創作が可能になる。さらにフレーバーキャビアの配合割合を変えると膨大な組み合わせになり、鍋に飽きるヒマがないかもしれない。

　球状化は、多くの人々が「分子調理法」と聞いた時に連想する技術のひとつであろう。この技術によって、イクラやキャビアのように、薄い膜の中に液体を含む球体を作ることができる。この球体は、独特の食体験をもたらす。すなわち、口腔内でつぶすと、膜の破裂によって液体が一気にはじけ出る感覚である。

　球状化の原理は、アルギン酸とカルシウムイオンの反応により薄膜が形成される、ゲル化の現象である。膜に内包される溶液にアルギン酸ナトリウムなどを溶かし、それをスポイトやスプーンを用いて乳酸カルシウムなどのカルシウムイオンを含む溶液中に滴下すると、分子キャビアが形成される。

　球状化が起こるメカニズムは、「エッグボックスモデル」とよばれている（図3-1）。卵のパックに相当するポリマーのアルギン酸の間に、卵に相当するカルシウムイオンが入り、アルギン酸同士を架橋して、ゲルを形成するというものである。

In mizutaki, the ingredients are boiled in hot water to bring out the natural flavors and served in a pot at the table. Adding extra seasoning such as ponzu sauce is an excellent way to enhance those flavors. It is popular to use condiments such as spring onions, grated daikon, chili, and yuzukoshou to change the taste while eating the hot pot dish.

In this recipe, liquid seasonings such as soy sauce, miso flavor sauce, kimchi flavor sauce, and sesame sauce are encased in a sphere. The flavor caviar can give mizutaki not only the flavors of the seasonings but also a popping texture. It is also easy to make complex flavors such as soy sauce caviar and kimchi caviar to create soy-sauce-kim-chi flavor, or miso and sesame to create miso-sesame flavor. Three types of flavor caviars can make seven ways combinations, 15 ways for four types, 31 ways for five types, and so on. Furthermore, changing the blending ratio of flavor caviar allows for a huge number of combinations. You may never get bored eating hot pot.

Spherification is one of the most well-known molecular cooking technologies. This technique can create spheres with a liquid in a thin membrane such as caviar or salmon roe. The spheres provide a unique eating experience. When you break it in your mouth, it feels like the liquid pops out into the mouth.

The principle of spherification is the gelling phenomenon, in which a thin gel membrane is formed through the reaction of alginate and calcium ions. Specifically, the alginate is dissolved in a solution encapsulated in the sphere. When the alginate solution is dropped into a solution containing calcium ions, molecular caviar is produced.

The mechanism that triggers spherification is called the "eggbox model" (Figure 3-1). In the model, calcium ions as eggs fit into the gaps of the alginate polymers as the eggbox, causing the alginates to cross-link with each other, and then the gel is formed.

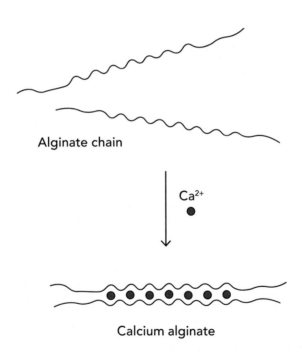

Alginate chain

Ca^{2+}

Calcium alginate

図3-1. カルシウムとアルギン酸ゲルのエッグボックスモデル
Figure 3-1. Eggbox model in calcium-alginate gels

　　　　　分子調理の日本食 ｜ Molecular Cooking in Japanese Cuisine

お 吸 い 物 球 体

Spherical Japanese clear soup

箸でつまんだ露の玉は、あさりとみつばの具が入った吸い物だ。球体を口に含んで舌の上で割ると、途端にだし汁のうま味が広がる。ほんのひとくちで満ち足りる汁物である。

大きなサイズの球体を作るには、アルギン酸塩を溶かした溶液を、カルシウム水溶液の中に注意深く浮かべるという方法がある。膜が張りめぐらされないうちに、丸い形をうまく整えられるならば、いろいろな具を包み入れた球体を作ることができる。

The dewdrop pinched with chopsticks is a clear soup with asari clam and mitsuba. Place the sphere in your mouth and break it on your tongue. Umami of the soup fills your mouth. You can fully enjoy the savoriness of the soup with just one sphere.

One way to make a large sphere is to float an alginate solution into a calcium solution carefully. Creating a round shape of the alginate solution before the membrane forms make it possible to get a sphere that encases various ingredients.

材料

- ・あさり…4個
- ・乳酸カルシウム…15g
- ・アルギン酸ナトリウム…8g
- ・かつお節…8g
- ・酒…5ml（小さじ1）
- ・みつば…4g
- ・乾燥こんぶ…3g
- ・薄口しょうゆ…2.5ml（小さじ1/2）

道具

- ・鍋
- ・菜箸
- ・こし器
- ・ボウル
- ・おたま
- ・網しゃくし
- ・ブレンダー

手順

1. あさりを沸騰しているお湯に入れ、身を取り出す。みつばは軽く洗ってから2cm幅に切る。

2. 鍋に水400mlとこんぶを入れ、弱火で加熱する。沸騰前にこんぶを取り出す。

3. ②にかつお節と酒を加え、中火で加熱する。沸騰後1分加熱してから火を止め、こし器でかつお節を除き、ボウルにだし汁を取る。薄口しょうゆを加え、すまし汁にする。

4. ③のすまし汁300mlにアルギン酸ナトリウムを添加し、ブレンダーで混ぜる。

5. 水500mlに乳酸カルシウムを溶かす。白色沈殿物がなくなるまで、よくかき混ぜる。

6. お玉で④を40mlすくい、その中にあさり2個とみつば2gを入れる。

7. ⑤の乳酸カルシウム水溶液に⑥をゆっくり落とす。

8. 溶液中で約1分間保持した後、網しゃくしで引き上げる。水で軽く流す。

③

4

4

INGREDIENTS

- 4 asari clams
- 15 g calcium lactate
- 8 g sodium alginate
- 8 g dried bonito flakes
- 5 ml (1 teaspoon) cooking sake
- 4 g mitsuba (Japanese parsley)
- 3 g dried kombu
- 2.5 ml (1/2 teaspoon) light soy sauce

UTENSILS

- pot
- cooking chopsticks
- strainer
- bowl
- ladle
- skimmer
- blender

STEPS

1. Boil and shuck asari clams. Rinse mitsuba in water and cut into 2 cm long pieces.

2. Put 400 ml of water and dried kombu in a pot and heat on low. Remove the kombu before boiling.

3. Add dried bonito flakes and cooking sake to #2 and heat on medium. Heat for 1 minute after it brings to a boil, turn off the heat, remove the bonito flakes with a strainer, and transfer the dashi stock into a bowl. Add light soy sauce to the stock to make a transparent soup.

4. Add sodium alginate to 300 ml of #3 and mix with a blender.

5. Add calcium lactate to 500 ml water. Mix well till the white precipitate dissolves.

6. Scoop 40 ml of #4 with a ladle and place two asari clams and 2 g of mitsuba into it.

7. Submerge #6 slowly in the calcium lactate solution (#5).

8. Leave the sphere in the solution for about 1 minute, and then scoop it up with a skimmer.

6

7

8

解説
Explanation

あらゆる"液体"を包むことができる
Any liquids can be encased.

　　球状化の技術を使うと、イクラのような小さい球体だけではなく、大きな球体も作ることができる。すまし汁にアルギン酸ナトリウムを溶かし、おたまですくってあさりとみつばを入れ、乳酸カルシウムの水溶液に静かに沈めれば、具を内包した球体の吸い物になる。

　　透明な液体の中にあさりとみつばが浮かぶ美しい見た目もさることながら、口の中で膜が弾ける食感とその後に広がる風味の感覚も新しい。液体でもあり固体でもある、風変わりな吸い物である。

　　球体の膜の強度は、カルシウムイオンの濃度、液体の酸性度、アルコールを含むかどうかなどに依存する。たとえば、アルギン酸塩を溶かした液体がpH5未満である場合、アルギン酸とカルシウムイオンとの結合は不十分となり、しっかりした膜が形成されにくくなる。100%りんごジュースのpHは3.6程度であるため、そのままでは球状化があまり上手くいかない。しかし、pHを上昇させるクエン酸ナトリウムなどをりんごジュースに添加することによって、改善することができる。

　　また、球体をカルシウムイオン水溶液に入れたままにしておくと、カルシウムイオンが球体内に拡散し、球体はすべて固体になる。そのため、膜が固くなりすぎないようにするには、球体を適切なタイミングで純水に移して、過剰なカルシウムを除去しなければならない。

　　乳製品のように、内液となる溶液にカルシウムイオンがもともと含まれている場合、アルギン酸ナトリウムを溶かす操作中に溶液が固まってしまう。このような場合、「逆球状化」を行うことで問題を解決することができる。これは、球体の内側の溶液ともう一方の溶液を逆にする方法である。すなわち、カルシウムイオンが豊富な牛乳などの乳製品を、アルギン酸塩水溶液の中に滴下して、膜を形成させるというものだ。逆球状化で作られる膜は、通常の球状化によって形成された膜よりも厚くなりやすいため、口の中でつぶしにくく、口当たりがあまり良くない。一方で、成形しやすいことや、提供する直前ではなく、作ってからある程度置いておくことができるなどの利点がある。逆球状化はまた、酸性の液体やアルコールなどを球体にしたい場合にも使える方法である。

The spherification technique can produce not only small caviar-sized spheres but also large spheres. It is also possible to encapsulate the ingredients of soup into the sphere. Place the asari clam and mitsuba in the ladle filled with the soup of sodium alginate, and submerge it gently in a calcium lactate solution.

The appearance of the clams and mitsuba floating in the transparent liquid is impressive. Another remarkable point is that the sphere bursts in the mouth and the flavor of the soup spreads out. It is an eccentric soup that is both liquid and solid.

The strength of the membrane depends on the concentration of calcium ions and the acidity and the alcohol content of the internal liquid. When the liquid in which the alginate is dissolved has a pH of less than 5, the binding of alginate and calcium ions will be insufficient, and the gel membrane formation is difficult. For example, 100% apple juice is not a suitable ingredient for spherification as its pH is about 3.6. In that case, a pH adjuster such as sodium citrate can enable membrane formation.

When the spheres are left in a calcium ion solution for a while, the calcium ions will diffuse into the spheres, and the whole sphere will solidify. The spheres must be transferred to pure water at an appropriate time to wash off any remaining calcium ions to prevent this from happening.

If the internal liquid solution originally contains calcium ions, as with dairy products, the solution solidifies during the procedure to dissolve sodium alginate. In such cases, the problem can be solved by "reverse spherification," a method of reversing the solutions for the inside and outside of the sphere. In other words, a solution rich in calcium ions is dropped into an aqueous alginate solution to be spherified. The membranes formed by reverse spherification tend to be thicker than those by normal spherification. As a result, it is harder to rupture in the mouth and is less palatable. On the other hand, the method has the advantages of ease of shaping, and the spheres can be stored for some time. This method is also suitable to create spheres with acidic or alcoholic liquids.

分子調理の日本食 ｜ Molecular Cooking in Japanese Cuisine

色 が 変 わ る 卵 か け ご は ん

Color-changing TKG

簡単な日本食メニューのひとつに、新鮮な生卵をごはんにかけて食べる「卵かけごはん」がある。

ここでの料理は卵の白身に“黄身のようなもの”をのせた、合成の卵かけごはんだ。黄身は球状化の方法で作った、ほろ苦い味がするターメリック入りの球体である。作りたての球体の色は、ターメリックの鮮やかな黄色だ。この球体を卵の白身の上にのせると、黄身の色は、てっぺんに向かってグラデーション状に赤みを帯びていく。アルカリ性の白身とターメリックのクルクミンが反応しているからだ。

しばらくは黄身を崩さずに、じわじわと色味の変化を味わっていたい卵かけごはんだ。

One of the simplest Japanese dishes is "tamago kake gohan," popularly abbreviated TKG. It is a dish in which a raw egg is put on top of or mixed into the rice.

The dish in our recipe is a synthetic tamago kake gohan with an egg yolk-like substance on an egg white and rice. The "yolk" is a slightly bitter-tasting sphere made by spherification. It contains turmeric to produce the yellow hue. When the yolk sphere is put on top of the egg white, the yellow color gradually becomes red from the bottom to the top because of the chemical reaction between curcumin in the turmeric and the alkaline egg white.

You will want to savor the gradual change in color without breaking the yolk and eating it.

材料

- ・炊飯米…180 g
- ・卵白…35g（1個分）
- ・乳酸カルシウム…15g
- ・ターメリック…4g
- ・アルギン酸ナトリウム…0.4g

道具

- ・ボウル
- ・おたま
- ・網しゃくし
- ・ブレンダー

手順

1. 水20mlにターメリックを加える。

2. ①にアルギン酸ナトリウムを添加し、ブレンダーで攪拌する。

3. 水500mlに乳酸カルシウムを溶かす。白色沈殿物がなくなるまでよくかき混ぜる。

4. おたまで②を③に入れ、溶液中でかたちを整える。

5. 乳酸カルシウム水溶液中に約2分間置いてから、網しゃくしですくい、水で軽く洗う。

6. お椀に炊飯米を盛り、卵白を載せる。

7. ⑥の卵白の上に⑤を載せる。ターメリックの球体が卵白と反応し、次第に赤くなる。

INGREDIENTS

- · 180 g cooked rice
- · 35 g egg white (pasteurized egg)
- · 15 g calcium lactate
- · 4 g turmeric
- · 0.4 g sodium alginate

UTENSILS

- · bowl
- · ladle
- · skimmer
- · blender

STEPS

1. Add turmeric to 20 ml of water.

2. Add sodium alginate to #1 and mix with a blender.

3. Put calcium lactate into 500 ml of water. Mix well till the white precipitate dissolves.

4. Submerge #2 in the calcium lactate solution (#3) with a ladle and shape it into a round.

5. Leave the sphere in the solution for about 2 minutes. Scoop it with a skimmer and rinse with water.

6. Serve cooked rice in a bowl and put the raw egg white on it.

7. Place #5 on top of the egg white (#6). The turmeric sphere will react with the egg white and its color gradually turn from yellow to red.

2

2

4

5

6

7

球状化 | Spherification

時間によって色が変化する"卵黄"とは？
Why does the color of the "egg yolk" change over time?

ターメリック（ウコン、学名 *Curcuma longa*）は、ショウガ科の多年草で、インドが原産地とされている。すこし土くささを感じさせる独特の香りやほろ苦い味、鮮やかな黄色が特徴的である。カレーパウダーには欠かせないスパイスだ。

このターメリックを焼きそば麺に振りかけると、麺は真っ赤に変わる。これはターメリック中に入っている黄色い成分のクルクミンが、焼きそば中のアルカリ性成分によって赤色の化学構造に変化するからである（図3-2）。

アルカリ性の食材はほとんどない。焼きそばなどの中華麺がアルカリ性なのは、かん水（炭酸ナトリウムや炭酸カリウムなど）というアルカリ塩を製麺工程で添加しているからである。天然でほぼ唯一ともいえるアルカリ性の食材は、卵の白身、卵白である。卵白は産卵直後の状態では中性～弱アルカリ性であるが、数日置くとpHが9以上のアルカリ性になる。これは、

卵白に含まれている酸性物質の二酸化炭素が揮発して殻から出ていくことで、卵白がアルカリ性に傾くからである。

以上の性質と球状化の技術を組み合わせることで、"色が変わる卵黄"を作ることができた。ターメリック水溶液を球状化したものを、本物の卵から取り出した卵白の上に載せると、卵黄の色はすぐに赤に変わるのではなく、卵白に接している箇所から徐々に赤くなっていく。条件により時間の違いはあるが、5分程度で球体全体が赤く染まった。

このレシピで作った"黄身"はターメリックの風味が強烈なので、正直なところ、本物の卵かけごはんの複雑なおいしさにはかなわない。しかし、合成卵黄は、成分の調製が自在にできるのが強みである。使うスパイスや調味料などを変えることで、バラエティに富んだ黄身を生むことができるだろう。

Turmeric (*Curcuma longa*) is a perennial plant in the ginger family Zingiberaceae and is native to India. It has characteristic earthy aroma, bitter taste, and vivid yellow color. It is the essential spice for curry powder.

When the turmeric is sprinkled on the yakisoba noodles, the noodles turn color from cream to bright red because curcumin, the yellow component in turmeric, is transformed into a red chemical by the alkaline component in the yakisoba noodles (Figure 3-2).

There are a few alkaline ingredients. The yakisoba noodles are alkaline because kansui is added to the noodle-making process. Kansui is a solution of alkali salt, such as sodium carbonate or potassium carbonate, which gives texture, flavor, and color to the noodles. One of the only naturally alkaline ingredients is egg white. The pH of the egg white in a freshly laid egg is neutral to weak alkaline. After a few days, it turns alkaline with pH 9 or higher because carbon dioxide, an acidic component in egg white, volatilizes and escapes through the eggshell.

Combining the above properties and the spherification technique makes it possible to create a "color-changing egg yolk." When the turmeric-spherified yolk is put on a natural egg white, the color of the yolk does not change immediately but gradually turns red at the surface in contact with the egg white. Depending on the conditions, the whole yolk will turn red in about five minutes.

The "yolk" in this recipe has quite a strong turmeric flavor. The taste is not as good as real tamago kake gohan. However, the synthetic yolk can be easily prepared with components as desired. With various spices and seasonings, it is possible to create a variety of different egg yolks.

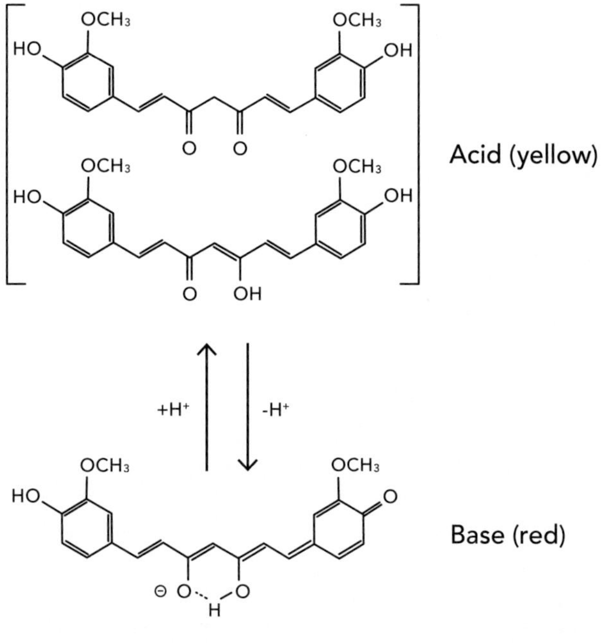

図3-2. 異なるpHでのクルクミンの化学構造と色の変化
Figure 3-2. Changing the chemical structure and the color of curcumin at different pH levels

食品に気体を入れ込むことで、その食感は軽く、風味は豊かになる。卵白のメレンゲのように泡立て器で空気を入れ込む方法以外にも、特殊な器具を使って二酸化炭素や亜酸化窒素のガスを食品に封入することができる。泡化・炭酸化の方法は、気体さえも食材にする。

4

泡化、炭酸化
Foaming and Carbonation

Through the addition of gas to food, the texture becomes lighter, and the flavor becomes richer. Besides adding air into a mixture with a whisk, as when making an egg white meringue, carbon dioxide and nitrous oxide gas can be injected into foods with special equipment. The method of foaming and carbonation turns the gas into an ingredient.

分子調理の日本食 | Molecular Cooking in Japanese Cuisine

(Recipe _ 10)

蕎麦プーマ

Soba-puma

エスプーマの登場で、あらゆる食材を素材の風味を生かしたまま泡立てることができるようになった。エスプーマとは分子調理の革命的な器具であり、調理法であり、泡料理の名前でもある。

できたての泡の料理を食べると、食感の面白さだけでなく、食材の香りを堪能することができる。

蕎麦のエスプーマ、すなわち「蕎麦プーマ」を、「蕎麦切り」の前菜として、ひとさじだけいただく。作りたての泡で香りを味わうと、蕎麦切りへのおいしい期待が膨らんでくる。さらに「蕎麦がき」をコースメニューに加えて、蕎麦の味をしっかり感じてみるのも良い。蕎麦のシンプルなおいしさを、五感で楽しむ方法だ。

With the advent of the Espuma, most ingredients can be made into foam, with the retention of flavors. Espuma is the name of the revolutionary molecular cooking equipment, the cooking method, and the dishes.

Freshly made foam will amuse you not only because of the fluffy mouthfeel but also the flavor of the ingredients.

Have a spoonful of "soba-puma" as an appetizer. The flavor of buckwheat released from the freshly made foam enhances your expectation for the main dish, "soba-kiri." To get the strong taste of buckwheat, you can add "soba-gaki" to the menu. This course meal is a way to fully enjoy soba-dishes made from virtually a single ingredient, buckwheat flour, using all five senses.

材料

・水 … 200ml
・蕎麦粉 … 12 g

道具

・小鍋
・泡だて器
・へら
・ボウル
・亜酸化窒素用エスプーマボトル
・亜酸化窒素ボンベ

手順

1. 小鍋に水200mlを入れ、蕎麦粉を加え、泡立て器でよく混ぜる。

2. とろみがつくまでかき混ぜながら、中火で5分間加熱する。

3. 粗熱をとった②を、亜酸化窒素ガス用のエスプーマボトルに入れ、ボトルヘッドをしっかりと締める。

4. 亜酸化窒素ガスを注入する。

5. すぐに30回ほどボトルを上下に振る。冷蔵庫で1時間静置する。

6. 60℃程度のぬるま湯でボトルを湯煎し、エスプーマボトルを温める。ノズルを下に向けてレバーを握り、エスプーマを出す。

INGREDIENTS

・200 ml water
・12 g buckwheat flour

UTENSILS

・small pot
・whisk
・spatula
・bowl
・espuma bottle for nitrous oxide
・nitrous oxide cylinder

STEPS

1. Add buckwheat flour to 200 ml of water in a small pot, and mix well with a whisk.

2. Heat on medium for 5 minutes while stirring until thickened.

3. When the mixture (#2) cools down, put it in an espuma bottle for nitrous oxide and tighten the bottle head firmly.

4. Inject nitrous oxide gas into the bottle.

5. Immediately shake the bottle up and down about 30 times. Place in the refrigerator for 1 hour.

6. Warm the bottle in hot water around 60℃ (140°F). Squeeze the lever with the nozzle facing down to release the espuma.

2

3

4

6

6

料理の世界に革命を起こしたエスプーマとは？
Espuma revolutionized the culinary world.

蕎麦といえば、細長い麺状の「蕎麦切り」が一般的だ。この蕎麦切りは16〜17世紀に日本で発明され、江戸時代中期には庶民の生活に広がった。それ以前の蕎麦料理といえば、蕎麦粉にお湯を入れ、こねて餅状にした「蕎麦がき」であった。

今回作ったのは、蕎麦粉をお湯で薄く溶かした液にエスプーマを使ってガスを封入した「蕎麦プーマ」だ。蕎麦がきから蕎麦切りが生まれた時以来の、ある種"蕎麦の大変革"といったら大げさだろうか。蕎麦粉が、餅状から麺状になり、さらに泡状になるという"進化"である。

エスプーマは、スペイン人のシェフ、フェラン・アドリア氏によって開発された調理法のひとつで、スペイン語で「泡」を意味している。この調理器具を使えば、通常泡立たない食材、例えばグリンピースやハーブなどの泡も作ることができる。

エスプーマに使用されるガスには、二酸化炭素（CO_2）と亜酸化窒素（N_2O）がある。二酸化炭素の場合は、シュワシュワとした食感に加え、わずかな酸味や苦味が食品へ付与される。つまり、二酸化炭素で作ったエスプーマは食品の味を若干変化させるため、利用できる範囲が限られる。それに対して、亜酸化窒素で作ったエスプーマは、食材のもともとの風味に大きな影響を与えない。

亜酸化窒素ガスは、諸外国では古くからクリームの発泡剤用の食品添加物として認められており、広く利用されてきた。日本では2005年に食品添加物として認められた。亜酸化窒素は使用許可を受けた飲食店などで利用することができ、家庭では使用が難しい。一方、二酸化炭素ガスはカートリッジのかたちで一般家庭向けに販売されている。

今回作った蕎麦のエスプーマは、亜酸化窒素ガスを使ったものである。この蕎麦プーマの特徴のひとつは、通常の蕎麦切りと比べて香りを味わうことに特化しているということだ。泡にすることで、蕎麦の香りをより強く感じることができる。

The current soba noodles are accurately named "soba-kiri." This dish was invented in Japan between the 16th and 17th centuries and popularized in the 18th century (Edo period). Before that, the typical soba dish was not a noodle but a dumpling of buckwheat called "soba-gaki."

The newly created dish is a "soba-puma," a foam of buckwheat filled with gas by espuma to the buckwheat flour and hot water mixture. It could be said there has been an evolution of buckwheat from a dumpling to a noodle and then to a foam.

Espuma is one of the cooking methods invented by Spanish chef Ferran Adrià and means foam in Spanish. The equipment makes it possible to produce foams from ingredients that generally do not foam, such as green peas and herbs.

The gases used in espuma are carbon dioxide (CO_2) and nitrous oxide (N_2O). Carbon dioxide imparts a little sourness and bitterness to the food, in addition to a fizzy texture. This means that carbon dioxide will slightly change food taste, so its range of use is limited. In contrast, nitrous oxide does not significantly affect the original flavor of the ingredients.

In Japan, nitrous oxide gas was approved as a food additive in 2005. It has long been recognized and widely used as a cream foaming agent in other countries. Nitrous oxide can be used in licensed restaurants, but it is difficult to use at home. On the other hand, carbon dioxide is sold in gas cartridges for home use.

The soba-puma is made with nitrous oxide gas in this recipe. One of this dish's characteristics is the special aroma of buckwheat flour compared to soba noodles. The foaming creates a stronger sense of the flavors of the ingredients.

スパークリング手巻き寿司

Sparkling hand-rolled sushi

視覚と記憶の思い込みを覆したいときは、この手巻き寿司を試してみるといいかもしれない。一見、何の変哲もないが、一口食べると脳みそがスパークするような刺激的な手巻き寿司だ。

口の中で寿司から炭酸が弾け出す。エスプーマを使って寿司ネタやシャリの中に二酸化炭素のガスを封入してあるからだ。シャリはお酢を使っていないが、二酸化炭素のガスを封入したことで、ほのかな酸味と苦味が感じられる。

「スパークリングいくら」は、主役級のインパクトがある。それは膜の「固体」と、中身の「液体」と「気体」を実感できる、ハイブリッド型の寿司ネタと言えるかもしれない。

If you want to overturn your visual and memory assumptions, try this hand-rolled sushi. At first glance, it looks like ordinary sushi, but one bite of this exciting sushi will spark your brain with amazement.

The fizzy carbonic acid pops out from the sushi in your mouth because carbon dioxide gas is sealed by espuma in the sushi toppings and rice. Although the sushi rice is not made with vinegar, the carbon dioxide gas is injected into the rice, which gives it a subtle sourness and bitterness.

Among these sushi toppings, "sparkling ikura" could be a star. It would be a hybrid type of sushi ingredient that makes you realize the membrane as the "solid" and the contents as the "liquid" and "gas."

材料

- ・炊飯米…300g
- ・ねぎとろ…150g
- ・サーモン…150g
- ・卵焼き…100 g
- ・きゅうり…70g
- ・いくら…50g
- ・砂糖…27g
- ・塩…4g
- ・焼きのり…大判4枚
- ・しそ…6枚

道具

- ・菜箸
- ・しゃもじ
- ・スプーン
- ・ボウル
- ・二酸化炭素ガス用エスプーマボトル
- ・炭酸ガスカートリッジ

手順

1. 水50mlに砂糖と塩を入れ、よく混ぜ合わせたものを、炊きたての炊飯米に全体にふりかけ、しゃもじで切るように混ぜ合わせる。

2. エスプーマボトルに①を入れる。

3. ボトルヘッドをしっかりと締める。二酸化炭素ガスを注入する。

4. いくら、サーモン、ねぎとろ、長さを切りそろえた卵焼きやきゅうりをエスプーマボトルにそれぞれ入れ、③と同じ操作を行う。

5. すべてのエスプーマボトルを冷蔵庫で3時間静置する。

6. エスプーマボトルからガスを抜き、具材を器に取り出す。炭酸が抜けきらないうちに手早く手巻き寿司を作る。

INGREDIENTS

- 300 g cooked rice
- 150 g minced tuna
- 150 g salmon
- 100 g tamagoyaki
- 70 g cucumber
- 50 g ikura (salmon roe)
- 27 g sugar
- 4 g salt
- 4 large sheets nori
- 6 pcs shiso (perilla)

UTENSILS

- cooking chopsticks
- rice scoop
- spoon
- bowl
- espuma bottle for carbon dioxide
- carbonated gas cartridge

STEPS

1. Add sugar and salt to 50 ml of water and mix well. Sprinkle it over freshly cooked rice, and mix it with a rice scoop.

2. Put #1 into the espuma bottle.

3. Tighten the bottle head. Inject carbon dioxide into the bottle.

4. Put ikura, salmon, minced tuna, tamagoyaki, and cucumber into an espuma bottle individually. Follow the same step as #3.

5. Place the bottles in the refrigerator for 3 hours.

6. Remove the gas and take out the ingredients from the espuma bottle. Immediately make hand-rolled sushi and eat them because carbonic acid is removed after a while.

4

6

6

炭酸化が食品の固定観念を覆す
Carbonation overturns stereotypes of foods.

スパークリング手巻き寿司、その見た目はまったく普通の手巻き寿司に見える。しかし、食べたとたん目が見開く。シャリからもネタからもピリピリした刺激を感じるからだ。特にいくらは、膜が弾けた瞬間に炭酸の発泡する刺激が口の中にあふれ、何気なく食べたとき、見た目とのギャップから受ける衝撃は大きい。

いくらは、固体の膜に液体が閉じ込められた球体だが、そこにエスプーマで二酸化炭素のガスを封入した。すなわち、このスパークリングいくらは、固体、液体、気体の3つの状態を同時に感じる食べものである。

二酸化炭素をご飯に入れ込むことでできあがったスパークリングシャリには、新しい寿司飯としての可能性が感じられた。また、寿司酢に含まれる酢酸の代わりに、炭酸で軽い酸味を加えることができた。エスプーマを使って、酸味を加えることで、通常のすし酢に使われる食塩や砂糖の添加量を減らすこともできるだろう。

このネタやシャリの作り方はごく簡単で、液体の食材と同じようにエスプーマ専用の容器に食材を入れ、気体を封入する。食材の形状、硬さなどによって、二酸化炭素ガスが中に入り込む時間や量は異なる。

炭酸が含まれる食品の代表には炭酸飲料があるが、これは清涼飲料水の中でも一番多く生産されており、高い需要があることがわかる。炭酸が含まれている食品は大半が液体であり、固体に炭酸を意図的に含ませた食品は少ない。しかし、エスプーマによって固体食品に炭酸を入れることは可能であり、エスプーマの容器を使ってイチゴなどの果物を炭酸化させることはすでに行われている。一方で、果物以外の固形の食材に炭酸を入れたものは一般化していない。

今回、さまざまな手巻き寿司の食材を炭酸化させて試食したところ、食材ごとに炭酸の感じ方が異なることがわかった。シャリ、いくら、卵焼きに二酸化炭素を封入したものは、食べたときに炭酸刺激を十分感じた。一方、きゅうり、ねぎとろ、サーモンは同じ条件で二酸化炭素を入れても炭酸を感じにくかった。

"Sparking hand-rolled sushi" looks like typical hand-rolled sushi. However, there is an eye-opening surprise in one bite. Carbon dioxide gas bubbles pop out from both the sushi rice and the toppings. In particular, when ikura pops, the mouth is filled with stimulation by carbon dioxide. When the sushi is put in the mouth casually, a great shock comes from the gap between the familiar appearance and the unusual texture.

The sparkling ikura is made by injecting carbon dioxide gas into normal ikura, a sphere with a liquid trapped in the solid membrane. This ikura has all three states of solid, liquid, and gas at the same time.

The sparkling sushi rice has the potential as new sushi rice. Carbon dioxide gives a light sourness to the rice instead of acetic acid contained in sushi vinegar. It may be possible to reduce the amount of salt and sugar used in regular sushi vinegar.

The sushi rice and toppings are very easy to make, in the same way as the liquid ingredients placed into the espuma bottles that were filled with gas. Depending on the ingredient's shape and hardness, the time and amount of carbon dioxide gas entering the ingredient vary.

Carbonated beverages are a prime example of carbonated foods. They have one of the largest production volumes among soft drinks, and there is a high demand for them. The majority of the carbonated food products are liquid, and few solid foods are intentionally carbonated. However, espuma makes it possible to inject carbon dioxide into solid ingredients. Fruits such as strawberries are an example of solids carbonated with espuma, but the carbonation of solid foods other than fruits has not yet been generalized.

In this recipe, stimulation with carbon dioxide was different for each ingredient. Sushi rice, ikura, and tamagoyaki injected with carbon dioxide have a distinctly carbonated stimulus in the mouth. On the other hand, cucumbers, minced tuna, and salmon do not have an effervescent quality even when carbon dioxide was injected into those ingredients under the same conditions.

　　　分子調理の日本食 | Molecular Cooking in Japanese Cuisine

エアあんみつ

Air anmitsu

ふんわりとした泡のあんを口に入れると、炭酸がシュワシュワと弾ける。爽やかな口当たりのあんみつである。

あんの種類は2つある。ひとつは正統派の小豆あんに二酸化炭素を封入したことで、あんの甘さにほのかな酸味と苦味が加わった、大人びた味わいのあんみつだ。もうひとつは枝豆で作ったずんだあんに亜酸化窒素を合わせて、あんの独特な青っぽい風味がそのまま活かされるように仕上がっている。

増粘安定剤などを加えないで作るエスプーマの泡は、口溶けの良さと引き換えに、泡が消えるのが早いことが難点だ。しかし、このあんみつは泡が消えてなくなる前に、一瞬で食べ尽くしてしまえるほどおいしい。

After putting the fluffy, foamy sweet bean paste into the mouth, fine bubbles are released from the paste. This "air anmitsu" is a dessert that adds a refreshing texture to traditional anmitsu.

Two types of foamy bean paste are created in this recipe. One is the classic red bean paste with carbon dioxide. Carbon dioxide gives the paste a complex taste with a hint of sourness and bitterness. The other is the sweet zunda (green soybeans) paste with nitrous oxide. The paste retains the original grass-like flavor of young soybeans.

The drawback of espuma foam made with no thickening stabilizers is that the foam disappears quickly in return for a melt-in-the-mouth experience. However, this anmitsu is so delicious that you can eat it up in an instant before the foam disappears.

材料

- ・小豆こしあん … 100g
- ・ずんだあん … 100g
- ・白玉団子 … 60g（6個）
- ・寒天 … 40g
- ・好きなフルーツ … 適量
- ・赤えんどう豆（お好みで）

道具

- ・小鍋
- ・木べら
- ・裏ごし器
- ・ボウル
- ・二酸化炭素ガス用エスプーマボトル
- ・亜酸化窒素用エスプーマボトル
- ・炭酸カートリッジ
- ・亜酸化窒素ボンベ

手順

[小豆あんのエアあんみつ]

1. こしあんに水30mlを加え、練りながら中火で加熱し、液体のあんを作る。沸騰したら火を止め、粗熱をとる。

2. ①の液体のあんを二酸化炭素ガス用のエスプーマボトルに詰め、ボトルヘッドをしっかりと締める。

3. 二酸化炭素ガスを注入する。

4. 30回ほどエスプーマボトルを上下によく振る。冷蔵庫に1時間静置する。

5. 器に白玉団子、寒天、フルーツ、赤えんどう豆を盛り、その上にエスプーマをしぼり出す。

[ずんだあんのエアあんみつ]

1. ずんだあんに水30mlを加え、練りながら中火で加熱し、液体のずんだあんを作る。沸騰したら火を止め、粗熱をとる。

2. エスプーマボトル内で詰まらないよう、粒の粗いずんだあんを裏ごしする。

3. ②の液体ずんだあんを亜酸化窒素ガス用のエスプーマボトルに詰め、ボトルヘッドをしっかりと締める。

4. 亜酸化窒素ガスを注入する。

5. 30回ほどエスプーマボトルを上下によく振る。冷蔵庫に1時間静置する。

6. 器に具材を盛り、その上にエスプーマをしぼり出す。

小豆あんのエアあんみつ
Air anmitsu with sweet red bean paste

INGREDIENTS

· 100 g strained sweet red bean paste
· 100 g sweet zunda (green soybeans) paste
· 60 g shiratama dango (dumplings made from refined rice flour called shiratamako)
· 40 g agar jelly
· any fruit, as needed
· red peas, as you like

UTENSILS

· small pot
· wooden spatula
· strainer
· bowl
· espuma bottle for carbon dioxide
· espuma bottle for nitrous oxide
· carbon dioxide cartridge
· nitrous oxide cylinder

STEPS

Air anmitsu with sweet red bean paste

1. Prepare a liquid sweet bean paste. Add 30 ml of water to strained sweet red bean paste and heat on medium while mixing. When it boils, turn off the heat and let it cool.

2. Put #1 in the espuma bottle for carbon dioxide and tighten the bottle head.

3. Inject carbon dioxide into the bottle.

4. Shake the bottle up and down about 30 times. Place it in the refrigerator for 1 hour.

5. Serve shiratama dango, agar jelly, fruits, and red peas in a bowl and squeeze the espuma on top.

Air anmitsu with sweet zunda paste

1. Prepare a liquid sweet bean paste. Add 30 ml of water to sweet zunda paste and heat on medium while mixing. When it boils, turn off the heat and let it cool.

2. Strain the coarse-grained zunda paste to prevent clogging in the espuma bottle.

3. Put #2 in the espuma bottle for nitrous oxide and tighten the bottle head.

4. Inject nitrous dioxide into the bottle.

5. Shake the bottle up and down about 30 times. Place it in the refrigerator for 1 hour.

6. Serve the same ingredients like the sweet red bean anmitsu into a bowl and squeeze the espuma on top.

ずんだあんのエアあんみつ
Air anmitsu with sweet zunda paste

壊れやすい泡を長持ちさせるためには？
How to make fragile foam last longer?

舌の上を滑り落ちるようなサラッとしたあんに、エスプーマでガスを含ませると、さらに軽く、あっさりした泡状のあんになる。小豆のあんには二酸化炭素のガスを、ずんだのあんには亜酸化窒素のガスを封入した。小豆のエアあんみつは、炭酸がシュワシュワはじける食感のあんを、ずんだのエアあんみつは、香り高いふわふわした食感のあんをそれぞれ体験できる。

エアあんみつなどの泡は、液体の中に気体が分散したコロイドと呼ばれる状態にある。コロイドは通常は不安定であるため、泡は簡単に壊れやすい。泡の寿命は、気泡表面の構造、気泡のサイズ、そして気泡を囲む層の剛性や厚さなどといった特性の影響を受ける。

エアあんみつの気泡を安定させるには2つの方法がある。一つは、エスプーマ容器に入れる前の液体のあんにペクチンなどの増粘剤を入れ、液体の粘度を上げることである。これにより、泡中の気体を取り囲む"壁"が壊れにくくなり、気泡はより強固になる。もう一つは、界面活性分子による気泡表面の安定化である。界面活性分子とは、同じ分子内に親水性と疎水性の領域を両方持っているもので、牛乳や卵に含まれるタンパク質などがある。

たとえば、液状のあんに脱脂粉乳を添加してからエスプーマを作るとする。その気泡中では、脱脂粉乳中のタンパク質分子の親水性領域が水相表面に向き、疎水性領域が空気相と結びつくようになる。この作用によって、タンパク質は気泡の表面で自身を分割し、泡は無添加のものと比べてより長持ちする（図4）。ビールの泡は、ビール中に天然に存在する多数の界面活性分子（ホップの苦味成分だけでなく、麦芽とそれらの副産物由来のタンパク質も含む）により、その気泡は安定している。

When the gas is injected into a smooth liquid bean paste with espuma, the paste changes to a light foam; the air anmitsu, which is made with carbon dioxide with a sweet red bean paste, is refreshing and has the fizzy texture of carbon dioxide. The other air anmitsu, which uses nitrous oxide with a sweet zunda paste, has a grass-like aroma and fluffy texture.

Foams such as air anmitsu are gas dispersed in a liquid, which is called a colloid. Since colloids are usually unstable, foams are fragile. The lifetime of foam is affected by properties such as the structure of the bubble surface, the size of the bubbles, and the thickness and the stiffness of the layer surrounding the bubble.

There are two ways to stabilize the bubbles in the air anmitsu. One way is to increase the viscosity by adding thickeners, such as pectin, to the liquid bean paste before putting the mixture into the espuma bottle, making the bubbles stronger because the "wall" surrounding the gas in the foam is less likely to break down. The other way is to stabilize the surface of the bubbles with surface-active molecules or surfactants. These surface-active molecules have both hydrophilic and hydrophobic regions within the same molecule. They include the proteins found in milk and eggs.

For example, suppose that skimmed milk powder is added to a liquid bean paste before making an espuma. In the bubble, the hydrophilic region of the protein molecules in the skimmed milk powder faces the surface of the aqueous phase, and the hydrophobic region is bound to the air phase. The surface-active milk proteins remain at the air-liquid interface so that the foam lasts longer than the additive-free one (Figure 4). In beer foam, the bubbles are stabilized by many surfactants naturally present in beer, including the bitter components of hops and proteins derived from malt and their by-products.

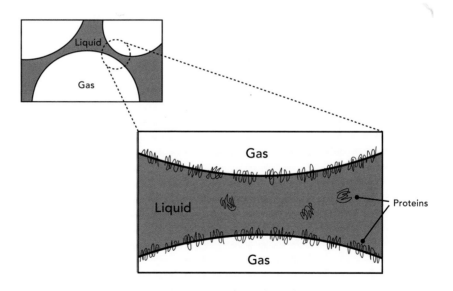

図4. 気泡の微細構造モデル
Figure 4. Microstructure model of foam

架橋化とは、橋を架けるように分子と分子の間を結合させることである。食材が化学結合でつながれることによって、従来とは異なる構造を持つ料理が構築される。トランスグルタミナーゼという酵素は、タンパク質の食品を架橋化することができ、その繋ぎ目は一見してもわからないほど自然だ。

5
架橋化
Cross-linking

Cross-linking is the binding reaction that links a polymer chain to another one. It is possible to create a dish that has an unconventional structure by connecting ingredients with chemical bonds. The enzyme transglutaminase can cross-link protein foods, and the linking area is so natural that they are not apparent at first glance.

分子調理の日本食 ｜ Molecular Cooking in Japanese Cuisine

(Recipe＿13)

ハイブリッド刺身

Hybrid sashimi

この奇妙な三色の刺身は、まぐろ、たい、サーモンで構成されている。とはいっても、新種のハイブリッド魚をさばいたのではなく、三種類の魚の切り身をトランスグルタミナーゼで接着したのだ。カラフルな見た目もさることながら、食感が複雑で、食べごたえのある刺身だ。

トランスグルタミナーゼは、タンパク質分子同士をたがいに結合させるはたらきを持つ酵素だ。さまざまな生物に存在しているが、食品加工の分野では、タンパク質の食材を接着させる"のり"としても使われる。この"のり"は共有結合でタンパク質分子をつなぎ合わせるので、三種類の魚がまるで一体化しているように見えるのだ。

This unique tricolor sashimi consists of raw tuna, sea bream, and salmon. However, it is not from a new species of crossbred fish but the fillets of the three fish bound together with transglutaminase. You will be satisfied with the colorful appearance of this sashimi as well as its complex texture.

Transglutaminase is an enzyme that binds protein molecules together. This enzyme is found in various organisms, and it is also used as a "glue" for protein ingredients in the field of food processing. The glue cross-links protein molecules using covalent bonds, so the three types of fish appear to be one piece.

材料

・まぐろ … 200g
・たい … 200g
・サーモン … 200g
・トランスグルタミナーゼ … 10g

道具

・包丁
・まな板
・茶こし
・バット
・ラップ
・食品用アルコールスプレー
・真空パック袋
・真空パック機

手順

1. まぐろ、たい、サーモンのサクをそれぞれ2本ずつ、同じ大きさの三角柱のかたちになるように切りそろえる。

2. バットにラップを敷き、その上に切り身を置き、食品用アルコールで表面をまんべんなく消毒する。

3. 茶こしを使って、切り身の表面にトランスグルタミナーゼを振りかける。

4. 切り身同士をしっかりと接着させる。

5. ラップでかたく包み、真空パック袋に入れ、真空パック機で脱気する。

6. 冷蔵庫内に約3時間おく。

7. 結着した部分の模様が出るように刺身を包丁で切る。

INGREDIENTS

・200 g tuna
・200 g sea bream
・200 g salmon
・10 g transglutaminase

UTENSILS

・kitchen knife
・cutting board
・tea strainer
・cooking tray
・plastic wrap
・food-grade disinfectant sanitizer
・vacuum-packaging bag
・vacuum-packaging machine

STEPS

1. Cut two pieces each of tuna, sea bream, and salmon fillets into equal-sized triangular prism shapes.

2. Place plastic wrap on a cooking tray. Place the fillets (#1) on it, and disinfect the surface of the fillets with food-grade disinfectant sanitizers.

3. Sprinkle transglutaminase on the surface of the fillets with a tea strainer.

4. Adhere firmly the fillets to each other.

5. Wrap #4 tightly in plastic wrap, put it in a vacuum-packing bag, and degas it with a vacuum-packing machine.

6. Place #5 in the refrigerator for about 3 hours.

7. Slice the combined fillet with a kitchen knife to make the tri-color sashimi.

トランスグルタミナーゼは"つなぎ合わせる"酵素
Transglutaminase is a "connection" enzyme.

まぐろとたいとサーモンの3種類の魚を結合した「ハイブリッド刺身」は、その食感がおもしろい。通常の刺身は、咀嚼中に魚肉の繊維に沿って一定の法則性で崩れていくのを感じるが、ハイブリッド刺身は、それぞれの魚の肉ごとの固さや舌の上での溶け具合などの変化が次々におとずれる。これは3種類の魚の刺身をいっぺんに咀嚼した時とは違った食感である。

食品のおいしさを増強させる反応に熟成がある。熟成は、魚よりも畜肉の方が一般的ではあるが、魚でも熟成させてうま味を引き出したり、食感を変えたりすることがよく行われている。熟成の反応は、高分子が分解し、それによって低分子が生成する方向に進む。具体的には、デンプンが分解することにより、甘味成分の単糖類が増加したり、タンパク質が分解することにより、うま味成分のアミノ酸が増えたり、脂質が分解することにより、独特の香り分子が生成したりする反応などである。

熟成に関わる反応には数々の酵素が関係している。食品成分を"ばらばらにする"酵素はたくさん知られているが、反対に、食品成分を"つなぎ合わせる"酵素は数が限られている。その酵素のひとつに、「トランスグルタミナーゼ」がある。

トランスグルタミナーゼは、主にタンパク質（グルタミン側鎖）とタンパク質（リジン側鎖）を共有結合でつなぎ合わせる（架橋化する）機能を持っている（図5）。微生物や動植物など自然界に幅広く存在する酵素で、特に動物の皮膚などに多く存在する。トランスグルタミナーゼによる架橋化反応により、皮膚表面の物理的強度や保湿機能が高まる。

食品業界では、放線菌が生産するトランスグルタミナーゼが発売されており、「食品物性の改良剤」として食品製造分野などで幅広く用いられている。トランスグルタミナーゼは、タンパク質同士を化学的につなぎ合わせ、多彩な食感をもつ料理を生み出す。「既存の素材の風味」と「斬新なテクスチャー」を実現するこの酵素は、現在、分子調理法の重要なツールとなっている。

トランスグルタミナーゼを使って、ハイブリッド刺身をつくる上で注意する点がある。それは、刺身の表層の細菌が刺身同士を合わせることによって内側に封じ込められ、内部で増殖するおそれがあることだ。食中毒を防ぐために、食品用アルコールなどで刺身の外側を消毒したあと、トランスグルタミナーゼで接着させる必要がある。

The "hybrid sashimi," which combines three types of fish, tuna, sea bream, and salmon, has an interesting texture. In this hybrid sashimi, the difference in the firmness and melting speed of each fish meat appears randomly as a change in texture.

The texture is entirely different than that felt when chewing three types of fish sashimi at once.

One of the reactions that enhances the deliciousness of food is aging. Aging is more common in livestock meat than in fish, but fish is also processed to bring out the flavor and tenderness.

In the reaction of aging, decomposition proceeds from macromolecules to small molecules. Specifically, there are several instances in the reaction: the breakdown of starch into monosaccharides of sweetness components, the breakdown of protein into amino acids of umami components, and the breakdown of fats and oils into unique flavor molecules.

A lot of enzymes are involved in the aging reaction. Among them, many are known to break down the components in food. In contrast, only a few enzymes can merge food components at the molecular level. One of those enzymes is transglutaminase.

Transglutaminase connects proteins (glutamine side chains) and proteins (lysine side chains) by covalent bonds (Figure 5). This function is called cross-linking. The enzyme is found in many microorganisms, animals, and plants and animal skins in particular. The cross-linking reaction of the enzyme increases the physical strength and the moisturizing function of the skin surface.

Transglutaminase, produced by Actinomycetes, is now on the market and is widely used in the food manufacturing industry to improve properties and textures. The enzyme chemically combines proteins, thus creating various new dishes with new textures. It is possible to create a dish with an "innovative texture" while maintaining the ingredient's original flavor. Therefore, it currently becomes an important tool in molecular cooking technology.

One thing to keep in mind is the prevention of food poisoning when making hybrid sashimi with transglutaminase. The bacteria on the surface of the sashimi may be trapped inside when bonding the fillet together and then grow inside. It is necessary to disinfect the surface of the fillets before the treatment with transglutaminase to prevent this.

図5. トランスグルタミナーゼの架橋化反応
Figure 5. Cross-linking reaction of transglutaminase

イナゴハンバーグ

Grasshopper hamburger steak

照り焼きのタレがつややかなハンバーグは、昆虫のイナゴをその姿のまま接着して丸形に成型した、昆虫肉のハンバーグである。食感はクリスピーで、あとを引く香ばしいおいしさがある。牛ひき肉のハンバーグとは違ったおいしさだ。

食用昆虫は高タンパク質で、生産のしやすさなどの理由から、近年は畜肉に代わる食材として注目を浴びている。日本ではイナゴを佃煮などにして食べてきた歴史がある。

トランスグルタミナーゼを使うと、イナゴ個体の繊細なかたちを崩さずに、昆虫同士をしっかりとくっつけることができる。ただし、ワイルドな見た目に抵抗がある場合は、粉末などに加工するほうがいいだろう。

The hamburger steak glazed with teriyaki sauce is made from insect meat. The round patty is formed by whole grasshoppers adhered together. It has a crispy texture and a roasted shrimp-like flavor. The taste is different from that of a ground beef hamburger steak.

Edible insects have been attracting attention these days as alternatives to livestock meats because they are high in protein and easy to breed. In Japan, rice grasshoppers have a long history of being eaten in tsukudani, a preservable food boiled down in soy sauce.

The grasshoppers can be firmly adhered to each other using transglutaminase without breaking the delicate shape of the individual insects. However, if one is not comfortable with the wild appearance, it is better to powderize them.

材料

- イナゴ（ゆでたもの）… 80g
- 砂糖 … 40g
- だし汁 … 20ml（小さじ4）
- しょうゆ … 20ml（小さじ4）
- 酒 … 20ml（小さじ4）
- 油 … 15ml（大さじ1）
- トランスグルタミナーゼ … 4g
- 片栗粉 … 3g
- おろししょうが … 少々

道具

- フライパン
- はけ
- へら
- スプーン
- 菜箸
- バット
- 真空パック袋
- 真空パック機
- オーブン

手順

1. イナゴにトランスグルタミナーゼをまぶし、よく混ぜる。

2. 真空パック袋に①を40gずつハンバーグ型になるように詰め、真空パック機で脱気する。冷蔵庫内に一晩おく。

3. 袋から取り出し、はけで表面に油を塗る。

4. 160℃のオーブンで15分間焼く。

5. フライパンにだし汁、酒、おろししょうがを入れ、沸騰させる。

6. ⑤に砂糖、しょうゆを加えた後、水で溶いた片栗粉を加えてとろみをつける。

7. ⑥に④のイナゴハンバーグをいれ、タレをからめる。

1

2

3

INGREDIENTS

· 80 g rice grasshoppers, boiled
· 40 g sugar
· 20 ml (4 teaspoons) dashi stock
· 20 ml (4 teaspoons) soy sauce
· 20 ml (4 teaspoons) cooking sake
· 15 ml (1 tablespoon) oil
· 4 g transglutaminase
· 3 g potato starch
· a pinch of grated ginger

UTENSILS

· frying pan
· brush
· spatula
· spoon
· cooking chopsticks
· cooking tray
· vacuum-packaging bag
· vacuum-packaging machine
· oven

STEPS

1. Coat the grasshoppers with transglutaminase.

2. Put 40 g of #1 in a vacuum-packaging bag and shape it into a patty. Degas with a vacuum-packing machine. Place in the refrigerator overnight.

3. Take out the patty from the bag and apply the oil to the surface with a brush.

4. Roast #3 in an oven at 160℃ (320°F) for 15 minutes.

5. Prepare the teriyaki sauce. Put dashi stock, cooking sake, and grated ginger in a frying pan, and bring to a boil.

6. Add sugar and soy sauce to #5, and then put potato starch with water to thicken the mixture.

7. Dip the cooked grasshopper hamburger steak (#4) into the teriyaki sauce (#6) and serve on a plate.

何が昆虫食の受容を抑制するのか？
促進するのか？
What hinders or promotes the acceptance of insect foods?

トランスグルタミナーゼでつなぎ合わせたイナゴを焼き、照り焼きのタレをからめ、照り焼きハンバーグのように盛り付けた。このハンバーグ、目を近づけてよく見るとイナゴの"群衆"である。作り方のポイントは、トランスグルタミナーゼをふりかけたイナゴ同士を真空パック中で確実に密着させることである。そうすると接着面がきれいなハンバーグ型となる。食べてみると、イナゴのパリパリとした食感に、とろりとした照り焼きの甘辛さが合う。イナゴは草食性の昆虫であるため、草っぽい風味が強いが、照り焼きのようなしっかりした味付がそれを緩和してくれる。

2013年の国際連合食料農業機関（FAO）の報告がひとつのきっかけとなり、昆虫が家畜の代替タンパク質源として注目されている。昆虫は家畜と比べて環境負荷が少なく、飼料変換効率が高く、さらに栄養価が高い。しかし、昆虫が実際に一般的な食生活に普及するには多くの課題がある。これまでの日本の代表的な昆虫食として挙げられるのは、イナゴを醤油と砂糖で甘辛く煮た佃煮であるが、それ以外に目立った調理法はない。昆虫料理のバリエーションが少ないことは、昆虫食の普及が進まない要因のひとつである。

現状で、昆虫食を食べたいと思っている人の割合は低い。あるアンケートでは、回答者の80%以上が昆虫食の見た目で食べる気が失われると答えた。その一方で、加工・調理した昆虫食を食べて、一度ポジティブな食経験をすると、未加工の昆虫食を食べたいと思う人が増えるという研究結果もある。そのため、昆虫食の普及には、食材としての昆虫と料理とのマッチングが重要である。食材によって適切とされる料理や調理法があるように、それぞれの昆虫ごとの適切な加工・調理を見つけることが昆虫食の可能性を広げると考えられる。

イナゴを粉にしてハンバーグにすれば、見た目からくる抵抗感を払拭させることは簡単だろう。しかし、イナゴのその形のままの構造が、パリパリとした食感を生み出すのに役立っており、おいしさという観点からは必ずしも粉末化させることが良いとは限らない。昆虫食の加工・調理にはバリエーションが必要で、それには分子調理法が切り札となるかもしれない。

This hamburger steak was made by fusing grasshoppers using transglutaminase, cooking in the oven, and serving on a plate like a Japanese teriyaki hamburger steak. A closer look reveals that it is a group of grasshoppers. The key to making the smooth patty is compressing the grasshoppers treated with transglutaminase each other tightly in the vacuum-packaging bag. The crispy texture of the grasshopper patty goes well with the sweet-and-salty thick teriyaki sauce. Since grasshoppers are herbivorous insects, their flavor is peculiar grassy. The robust flavor of the teriyaki sauce softens the grasshopper flavor.

Insects are gaining attention as an alternative protein source for livestock, beginning with a report from the Food and Agriculture Organization of the United Nations (FAO) in 2013. Insects have a lower environmental impact, higher feed conversion efficiency, and higher nutritional value than livestock. However, there are many challenges to address before insects can become part of our daily foods. A typical insect food in Japan is tsukudani, simmered ingredients in soy sauce and sugar, but there have been no other notable dishes. This lack of a variety of insect-based foods is one reason why they have not become more popular.

Currently, a low percentage of people are willing to eat insect foods. In some surveys, more than 80% of respondents said that they lost their appetite because of the appearance of insects. On the other hand, the research has shown that once a person has a positive experience when eating processed and cooked insects, they are more likely to eat unprocessed insects. It is important to identify a good match between each insect and the type of cooking method or dish for acceptance of insect-based foods. Like other ingredients, the appropriate cooking methods and dishes for each type of insect will open up possibilities for insect-based diets.

If the hamburger steak is made from powdered grasshoppers, it would be easy to address the resistance resulting from appearance. However, the grasshopper's original structure produces a crispy texture, so powdering them is not the best solution in terms of deliciousness. Insect foods require variations in the processing and cooking methods, and molecular cooking technology would play a leading role in that regard.

分子調理の日本食 ｜ Molecular Cooking in Japanese Cuisine

かつお節酒器

Katsuobushi sake cup

　かつお節で作った器に日本酒を入れて飲む。かつお節の風味を日本酒がすこし含んで、お酒の深みがさらに増す。お望みならば、器のかつお節をつまみながら、ちびちびとお酒を楽しむこともできる。器がなくなってしまわないように注意が必要だ。

　この器はかつおの削り節をトランスグルタミナーゼで固めたものだ。かつお節は魚のかつおから作られる発酵食品である。日本で古くから作られてきた、だしのうま味を得るのに欠かせない、風味豊かなタンパク質の食材だ。

　歴史ある食材と新しい食材をシンプルに組み合わせて、「味わい深い食器」ができた。

Pour sake into the small cup made of katsuobushi, bonito flakes, and drink. The sake absorbs some of the flavors of the bonito flakes, which makes the sake even richer. You can sip the sake while taking a bite of the brim of the cup if you like, but you have to be careful not to eat too much of it.

Transglutaminase was used to firm the bonito flakes to form the cup. They are flavorful protein ingredients that have been made in Japan for a long time and are one of the essential ingredients used in dashi soup to give it an umami flavor.

A simple combination of the traditional and new ingredients results in the "tasteful cup."

材料

・かつお節 … 20g
・トランスグルタミナーゼ … 5g

道具

・茶こし
・バット
・ラップ
・スプレーボトル
・おちょこ
・真空パック袋
・真空パック機
・オーブン

手順

1. バットの上にラップを敷き、かつお節10gをラップのうえに平たく敷く。その上からスプレーボトルで水を吹きかけ、全体を湿らせる。

2. トランスグルタミナーゼを、茶こしを使って全体にふりかける。さらに水で全体を湿らせたのち、残りのかつお節10gを載せ、再度湿らす。

3. 型を取るためのおちょこをラップで包んだものを、②に載せてさらに包み、成型する。

4. ③を真空パック袋に入れ、脱気する。冷蔵庫で72時間おく。

5. 袋やラップを取り除き、型を外した後、100℃のオーブンで10分焼く。

INGREDIENTS

· 20 g katsuobushi (bonito flakes)
· 5 g transglutaminase

UTENSILS

· tea strainer
· cooking tray
· plastic wrap
· spray bottle
· sake cup
· vacuum-packaging bag
· vacuum-packaging machine
· oven

STEPS

1. Place plastic wrap on a cooking tray and lay 10 g of bonito flakes flat on the wrap. Spray water over it with a spray bottle to moisten the whole.

2. Sprinkle transglutaminase over the bonito flakes with a tea strainer. Spray water and spread the remaining 10 g of the bonito flakes on them. Spray water over them again.

3. Wrap a sake cup with plastic wrap. Place the wrapped cup on #2 and wrap it tightly.

4. Put #3 in a vacuum-packaging bag and evacuate the air. Place in the refrigerator for 72 hours.

5. Remove the bag, plastic wrap, and the sake cup. Bake the bonito flakes cup in an oven at 100℃ (212°F) for 10 minutes.

トランスグルタミナーゼで
食材を再構築する
Transglutaminase reconstructs ingredients.

　かつお節の主成分はタンパク質であるため、トランスグルタミナーゼでそのタンパク質の架橋化が可能である。ただし、かつお節は水分含量が低いため、トランスグルタミナーゼの粉末をふりかけただけでは酵素が反応せず、つながらない。水分を加え、酵素反応を進みやすくした条件でかつお節をおちょこ状に成形することで、架橋され、食べられる酒器ができる。架橋化した後、オーブンで水分を飛ばすと、かつお節酒器の見た目は、木肌のような質感になる。うまく作ると、くりかえし液体を入れても水分がしみ出さない。最後は、酒器も食べて、飲んだ跡形をなくすことができる。

　現在、トランスグルタミナーゼの利用が最も進んでいるのは、かまぼこなどの水産練り製品の加工分野である。これまでは、ナトリウムやカルシウムなどのミネラルが食感の改善に使われていたが、それらと違い、トランスグルタミナーゼは食材の風味には影響を与えないというメリットがある。

　このトランスグルタミナーゼが脚光を浴びたのが、食肉分野での利用であろう。ソーセージの皮の"バキッ"とした食感を向上させるだけでなく、例えば、バラバラの肉片にトランスグルタミナーゼの粉末をまぶし、ラップで包んで置いておくだけで、翌日には立派なステーキ肉になるというものである。変わった使い方としては、トランスグルタミナーゼを使って「エビが95％以上入ったパスタ」が作られており、別名「麺の再発明」とも言われた。

Since the main component of bonito flakes is protein, it is possible to combine the proteins by transglutaminase. However, the water content of bonito flakes is low, so additional water is needed to enable the enzymatic reaction. By sprinkling transglutaminase on moistened bonito flakes and molding them, the proteins are cross-linked, and the cup shape is formed. After the cross-linking reaction, the water in the bonito flakes is removed by oven heating, and then the surface of the cup becomes wooden-like. A well-made cup will not leak even if it is filled with liquid over and over again. The sake cup can be eaten, and all traces of drinking can be eliminated at the end.

Currently, the use of transglutaminase is most advanced in the processing field of fish paste products such as kamaboko fish cakes. So far, minerals such as sodium and calcium have been used to improve the products' texture. They can affect the flavor of the ingredients but transglutaminase does not.

Transglutaminase is also effectively utilized in the meat industry. This enzyme can improve the "snap" texture of sausages and turn multiple small meat pieces into one large steak meat. In an unusual use, a "pasta made from over 95% shrimp" was made with the enzyme. It was also known as the "reinventing of noodles."

乳化とは、水と油のように本来混じり合わない液体が均一に混合される状態のことである。混ざり合ったものはエマルションと言われ、スープやドレッシングなどによく見られる。分子調理法でエマルションを作るには、乳化剤や特殊な機械を使って混ぜる方法がある。

6

乳化
Emulsification

Emulsification is a state in which immiscible liquids, such as water and oil, are uniformly mixed. The mixture is called an emulsion and is often found in soups and dressings. In molecular cooking methods, one can use an emulsifier or a special machine to combine them to make emulsions.

飲むポテトサラダ

Drinkable potato salad

コップに注がれたのはポテトサラダだ。小さく切ったきゅうりやにんじんが、食感のアクセントとなっている。クルトンなどをトッピングしてもおいしいかもしれない。じゃがいものスープとは別物で、なめらかな口当たりの濃厚なポテトサラダの味がする。

飲むポテトサラダは、ムラのない液体に仕上がっているが、これは水分子と油分子が混ざり合っている「乳化」という状態になっているからだ。乳化を助ける乳化剤には、レシチンという脂質が使われている。レシチンは水と油のどちらとも親和性が高く、両者が混ざり合い、安定して存在するための仲介役になる。レシチンはマヨネーズやチョコレートなどにも使用されている、天然の食品成分である。

The potato salad was poured into a glass. Small chopped cucumbers and carrots accentuate the texture. It may be good with a topping like croutons. Unlike potato soup, it has a rich taste of Japanese-style potato salad with a creamy mouthfeel.

This potato salad is a smooth liquid with no grain because the liquid is in a state of emulsion, where water molecules and oil molecules are mixed. Lecithin, a type of lipid, is used as an emulsifier to stabilize the emulsion. Since lecithin has a high affinity for both water and oil, it acts as a mediator for mixing. Lecithin is a natural food ingredient used for mayonnaise and chocolate.

材料

- じゃがいも…40g
- にんじん…20g
- サラダ油…15ml（大さじ1）
- きゅうり…10g
- 大豆レシチン…4g
- コンソメ顆粒…2g
- 砂糖…1g
- 塩・コショウ…少々
- クルトン（お好みで）

道具

・小鍋	・耐熱ボウル
・包丁	・ゴムべら
・まな板	・ブレンダー
・スプーン	・電子レンジ

手順

1. 耐熱ボウルに大豆レシチンと水20mlを入れ、500Wの電子レンジで2分間加熱する。

2. ①に水75ml、サラダ油、コンソメ、塩、コショウを少々加え、ブレンダーで攪拌する。

3. ②に下茹でしたじゃがいもを加え、さらにブレンダーで攪拌する。

4. にんじんはさいの目に切って下ゆでする。きゅうりは小さく切る。

5. ④のにんじんやきゅうりを容器に移し、③を注ぐ。

INGREDIENTS

- 40 g potato
- 20 g carrot
- 15 ml (1 tablespoon) salad oil
- 10 g cucumber
- 4 g soy lecithin
- 2 g consommé granules
- 1 g sugar
- a pinch of salt
- a pinch of pepper
- crouton, as you like

UTENSILS

- heat-resistant bowl
- small pot
- kitchen knife
- cutting board
- spoon
- rubber spatula
- blender
- microwave oven

STEPS

1. Put soy lecithin and 20 ml of water in a heat-resistant bowl and heat in a microwave oven at 500W for 2 minutes.

2. Add 75 ml of water, salad oil, consommé granules, salt, and pepper to #1, and mix with a blender.

3. Add boiled potato to #2 and mix with a blender.

4. Dice and blanch carrots. Dice cucumbers.

5. Put #4 in a glass and pour #3 into it.

1

1

1

2

3

3

5

「固体の料理」を「液体の料理」に変えるには？
How can solid foods be turned into liquid foods?

　ホクホクとした固体のポテトサラダも、乳化剤であるレシチンを使うと、とろりとした液体の"飲むポテトサラダ"に変えることができる。液体のじゃがいも料理には、じゃがいもを煮て裏ごしし、生クリームで伸ばしたヴィシソワーズがあるが、飲むポテトサラダとヴィシソワーズの違いは、前者がポテト自体の風味をより感じられることである。

　乳化した状態の物質はコロイドの一種である。コロイドとは、「固体、液体、気体のいずれかの相の中に、別の相の粒子が分散はしているが、溶解はしていない状態のもの」だ。コロイドの種類には乳化の他に、懸濁液、ゲル、泡などがある。牛乳は、固体の乳タンパク質集合体であるミセルが液体である水に分散している懸濁液だ。反対に、ゼリーは、水が固体のゼラチンの中に分散しているゲルである。液体や固体の中に気泡がたくさん分散すると、泡の構造になる。液体の中に気体が入っている状態であるホイップクリームはリキッドフォームであり、固体の中に気体が入っている状態であるスフレやマカロンはソリッドフォームである。液体や固体に気体を入れることで、口あたりや口溶けが良くなる。

　水は例外として、食品の分子の多くは加熱により元の相から別の相へと変化する相転移があまり起こらない。相転移する前に、化学反応によって構造が違う分子になることが多いからだ。料理中の分子を相転移させるのは難しいが、料理の固体、液体、気体といった相を、乳化剤などを使って変化させるという発想は、新しい料理を開発する上で、ひとつのヒントになるだろう。

A solid potato salad can be transformed into a thick liquid potato salad by lecithin, an emulsifier. At first glance, it looks like vichyssoise, a pureed potato soup with cream, but it does not need cream to dissolve the potatoes. This dish's flavor is that of the potato salad itself, and it is different from a potato soup, which contains cream.

An emulsified substance is a type of colloid. A colloid is a mixture in which particles of one phase (solid, liquid, or gas) are dispersed but not dissolved in another phase. Suspensions, gels, and foams are also in this category. Milk is a suspension in which micelles, the solid milk protein aggregates, are dispersed in liquid water. Jelly is a gel in which liquid water is dispersed in solid gelatin. Foam is formed when a lot of air bubbles are dispersed in a liquid or solid. Whipped cream is liquid foam, a gas in a liquid, while soufflés and macaroons are solid foam, a gas in a solid. Putting gas into the liquid or solid foods improves the mouthfeel or melting feeling of the foods.

In most food molecules, except water, phase transitions (the change from one phase to another) do not often happen by heating because chemical reactions occur before the phase transition, and the molecules change to different structures. Therefore, the idea of using an emulsifier to change the three phases of dishes would be a breakthrough in the development of new dishes.

(Recipe _ 17)

さ ば の エ マ ル シ ョ ン 煮 三 種

Mackerel simmered in three kinds of emulsions

さばのみそ煮から発想を得た、さばのエマルション煮である。すなわち、レシチンで乳化させたエマルション液でさばを煮た料理だ。

エマルションとは液相に別の液相が分散しているものだ。この料理では、それぞれ「水＞油」、「水＝油」、「水＜油」の割合で調製したエマルション液を使っている。調理の過程で、それぞれのエマルション液に溶け出してくる物質の種類や量には違いがある。見た目では違いがわかりにくい、さばのエマルション煮だが、水が多い方には昆布の風味を、油が多い方にはねぎやしょうがの香りをより強く感じることができる。

さばは低温調理法を使って柔らかく仕上げている。低温調理法は、分子調理を世に広めることになった代表的な調理法のひとつである。

It is inspired by mackerel simmered in miso, which is one of the most traditional Japanese recipes. We simmered mackerel in an emulsion with lecithin instead of miso.

An emulsion is a liquid in which one liquid phase is dispersed in another phase. In our recipe, three types of emulsions are prepared in the following ratios: water > oil, water = oil, and water < oil. During the cooking process, different types and amounts of substances dissolve into each emulsion. Though there is almost no difference in the appearance of the dishes, the mackerel cooked with a higher water emulsion has a stronger flavor of kombu, while the emulsion with more oil has one of green onion and ginger.

The mackerel is tenderized using the sous vide cooking method, one of the typical techniques that have made molecular cooking known to the world.

材料

- さば … 200g
- アマニ油 … 150ml
- 長ねぎ … 60g
- しょうが … 30g
- 乾燥こんぶ … 9g
- 大豆レシチン … 3g

道具

- 耐熱ボウル
- 計量カップ
- スプーン
- 菜箸
- 深鍋
- ジッパー付保存袋
- 低温調理器
- 電子レンジ

手順

1. 耐熱ボウルに水20mlと大豆レシチンを入れ、500Wの電子レンジで2分間加熱する。加熱後、液を3等分する。

2. 計量カップを使って、水10ml＋アマニ油90ml、水50ml＋アマニ油50ml、水90ml＋アマニ油10mlの各溶液を作る。

3. ②に①をそれぞれ入れ、ブレンダーでよく攪拌し、乳化させる。

4. しょうがは皮をむき薄切りにし、ねぎは斜めに切る。さばを食べやすい大きさに6つに切り分ける。

5. ジッパー付保存袋に、長ねぎ、しょうが、こんぶをそれぞれ入れる。同じものを3袋用意する。

6. ⑤に③で乳化させたエマルション溶液をそれぞれ入れる。

7. さばの切り身を一袋あたり2切入れ、封をする。

8. 低温調理器で60℃に保温した湯に入れ、約1時間調理する。

9. 袋からさばを取り出し、一緒に加熱したこんぶや長ねぎなどと盛り付ける。

INGREDIENTS

· 200 g mackerel
· 150 ml flaxseed oil
· 60 g green onion
· 30 g ginger
· 9 g dried kombu
· 3 g soy lecithin

UTENSILS

· heat-resistant bowl
· measuring cup
· spoon
· cooking chopsticks
· deep pot
· zipper storage bag
· sous vide machine
· microwave oven

STEPS

1. Put soy lecithin and 20 ml of water in a heat-resistant bowl. Heat in a microwave at 500W for 2 minutes. Divide the liquid into three equal portions.

2. Prepare the solutions consisting of water and flaxseed oil in three different ratios: 10 ml water and 90 ml flaxseed oil, 50 ml water and 50 ml flaxseed oil, and 90 ml water and 10 ml flaxseed oil.

3. Add #1 to each solution (#2). Mix well with a blender to emulsify.

4. Peel and slice ginger. Cut green onion diagonally. Cut a mackerel fillet into six pieces.

5. Put green onion, ginger, and kombu in a zipper storage bag. Prepare three bags of the same.

6. Pour each of the emulsified solution (#3) into the bag (#5) individually.

7. Put two pieces of mackerel in each bag.

8. Heat all bags with the sous vide machine at 60°C (140°F) for about 1 hour.

9. Take out the mackerel fillets, kombu, and green onions from the bags and serve on plates.

6

7

8

エマルション×低温調理
＝新しい煮物
Combine sous vide with an emulsion
to get a new simmered dish.

　食材を水で煮れば水煮、油で煮ればオイル煮というが、水と油が均一に混ざった液体で煮るのは何と呼ぶべきか。水とアマニ油（栄養補助食品としての需要がある食用油）を1：9、5：5、9：1の割合でそれぞれ合わせ、レシチンで乳化させたエマルション中でさばを低温調理した。この調理法を名付けて「エマルション煮」とした。

　興味深いのは、できあがった料理の風味の違いである。水が多いエマルション煮のさばは、昆布の風味が強調され、油の多いエマルション煮のさばは、ねぎやしょうがの香りが強調されていた。水と油が同量のものは、昆布と薬味の風味をバランス良く感じられるものであった。

　本来、水と油は混じり合わず、同一容器に入れて激しく混合しても、しばらくすると両者は分離する。しかし、この時、双方に親和性を持つ乳化剤を入れておくと、エマルションが形成され混ざり合う。

　乳化剤となりうるものは、水になじむ親水性と油になじむ疎水性の性質を持っている両親媒性の分子である。天然の乳化剤には乳タンパク質などがあるが、食品加工でよく使用されているのは大豆と卵黄に含まれているレシチンである。さばのエマルション煮で用いた大豆レシチンは、卵黄レシチンより安価であるため、さまざまな食品に使われている。

　低温調理に正確な定義はないが、55〜90℃の温度帯でじっくり加熱する調理法のことを指す。低温調理は肉の調理によく用いられる。長時間加熱することで、肉のテクスチャーに大きく影響するコラーゲンのゼラチン化が起こり、肉が柔らかくなることが知られている。また、食材を真空パックして調理するため、食材のロスが少なく、大量調理が可能になるなど、さまざまな利点がある。今回のレシピでは、60℃の温度に設定したエマルション中でさばを1時間調理した。仕上がった魚の身は、とてもやわらかくジューシーであった。

Although there are ways to simmer fish with water or oil, fish is simmered in the water and oil homogeneous mixtures in this recipe. Water and linseed oil (cooking oil in demand as a dietary supplement) were mixed at a ratio of 1:9, 5:5, and 9:1; then, the mackerel was cooked with the three emulsions at low temperature. This cooking method was given the name "simmered in a emulsion."

What makes the three dishes interesting is the difference in the flavors. The mackerel with the emulsion in a high ratio of water had a stronger kombu flavor, and the one in a high ratio of oil had an emphasized green onion and ginger flavor. Furthermore, the one in the same ratio of water and oil had a well-balanced flavor.

Normally, water and oil do not remain evenly mixed. Even when they are mixed physically, they will separate after a while. However, if an emulsifier with an affinity for both is used, the two will mix, and the emulsion is formed.

Molecules that have both hydrophilic and hydrophobic properties are called amphipathic molecules. They can be used as emulsifiers. A typical example of natural emulsifiers is a milk protein. The common emulsifier in food processing is lecithin, found in soybeans and egg yolks. Soy lecithin, used in this recipe, is widely utilized in various food products, as it is less expensive than egg yolk lecithin.

There is no exact definition for sous vide cooking, but it refers to a slow cooking method at a temperature range of 55°C–90°C (131°F–194°F). Sous vide cooking is often used with meat. It is known to tenderize meat, as long heating gelatinizes the collagen, affecting meat texture. Sous vide cooking has several other advantages, such as the use of vacuum-packed ingredients, which reduces food loss and allows for mass cooking. In this recipe, mackerels were cooked in the emulsion at 60°C (140°F) for one hour. As a result, fish meat became very tender and juicy.

分子調理の日本食 ｜ Molecular Cooking in Japanese Cuisine

超音波乳化ラーメン

Ultrasonic emulsification ramen

オレンジ色のラーメンスープは塩スープとラー油でできている。超音波ミキサーを使って乳化させると、スープとラー油がよく混ざり合って、目にしみるほど鮮やかで辛いスープになった。

このスープの乳化状態は、水中に油の微粒子が均一に分散している「水中油滴型」である。超音波ミキサーを使った調理法は、食品添加物を使うことなく、強力に食材を混ぜ合わせたいときに利用できる。

このラーメンの油は、すぐにスープから分離しないので、あわてて麺をすすって辛さにむせることなく、じっくり味わえる。

The orange-colored ramen soup is made from salt-based broth and chili oil. The soup has a vivid color and spicy taste that stings the eyes, created by emulsifying the broth and chili oil with an ultrasonic mixer.

This soup's emulsification is an oil in water type, in which the oil particles are evenly dispersed in water. An ultrasonic mixer allows for the powerfully mixing of ingredients together with no food additives.

The oil does not immediately separate from the ramen soup, so you can savor it slowly without rushing to slurp up the noodles and choking on the spiciness.

材料

- ・ラー油 … 10ml（小さじ2）
- ・鶏ガラスープのもと … 7g
- ・和風だしのもと … 4g
- ・塩 … 3g
- ・ラーメンの麺と具材
  （長ねぎ、チャーシュー、半熟卵）

道具

- ・小鍋
- ・計量カップ
- ・おたま
- ・超音波ミキサー

手順

1. 小鍋に水500ml、鶏ガラスープのもと、和風だしのもと、塩を入れ、中火で沸騰させる。スープを計量カップに移す。

2. ①にラー油を加える。

3. 超音波ミキサーを使って、②に超音波を30秒ほど照射し、スープとラー油を乳化させる。

4. ラーメンの麺や具材などを盛り付けたどんぶりに③を注ぐ。

INGREDIENTS

- · 10 ml (2 teaspoons) chili oil
- · 7 g chicken stock concentrate
- · 4 g dashi stock concentrate
- · 3 g salt
- · ramen noodles and toppings
  (green onions, roast pork,
  and soft-boiled eggs)

UTENSILS

- · small pot
- · measuring cup
- · ladle
- · ultrasonic mixer

STEPS

1. Put 500 ml of water, chicken stock concentrate, dashi stock concentrate, and salt in a pot and heat on medium until it boils. Transfer the soup to a measuring cup.

2. Add chili oil to #1.

3. Using an ultrasonic mixer, irradiate #2 with ultrasonic waves for 30 seconds and emulsify the soup and chili oil.

4. Serve ramen noodles and toppings in a bowl and pour the emulsified soup (#3).

1

1

2

3

4

解説
Explanation

エマルションの中で何が起こっているのか？
What is the state of the emulsion?

ラーメンのスープと乳化は関係が深い。とんこつラーメンの白濁したスープは、さまざまな食材の成分が混ざり合い、乳化の状態になっている。一方で、通常、中華スープにラー油やごま油を後から加えると、油はスープの表面に浮いてしまう。スープと油を乳化させるには、レシチンのような乳化剤を使う化学的な方法もあるが、機械を用いた物理的な方法で乳化させることもできる。物理的な乳化に有効なのが、超音波である。

水と油が入った溶液に強力な超音波を照射すると、両者は短時間で混ざり合う。塩スープとラー油も超音波を使って乳化させると、1分も経たないうちに均一に混ざり合い、全体がオレンジ色のスープへと変わった。

また、超音波で乳化させた液体は、一般的なミキサーなどで撹拌したものと比べて分離しにくい。超音波ミキサーは、食品加工の分野でも分散・乳化・混合の目的で使用されており、マヨネーズやジュースなどの製造に使われている。

エマルションとは、水と油のような通常は分離する液体が混ざり合った状態のものを指すが、ただ混ざり合う混和とは異なる。エマルションは、乳化剤や超音波ミキサーなどを用いて、片方の液体をとても小さな小滴にして、もうひとつの液体中に分散させているものである。

これを応用したのがバターやマーガリンであり、ドレッシングやマヨネーズでもある。前者は油脂の中に水が分散している油中水滴型（W/O型：water in oil）のエマルションで、後者は水の中に油脂が分散している水中油滴型（O/W型：oil in water）エマルションである（図6）。バターでは、原料である牛乳中の脂質やリポタンパク質といった天然の乳化剤が、水を油脂中に分散することを助けている。

Ramen has a deep connection with emulsification. For example, the cloudy white soup of tonkotsu ramen is a emulsion of various ingredients. On the other hand, when chili oil or sesame oil is added to the soup later, the oil will float up the surface. There are two ways to mix the soup and the oil thoroughly. One is a chemical method; for example, using an emulsifier such as lecithin. The other is a physical method; for example, using machines such as an ultrasonic device.

When the water and oil solution is irradiated to powerful ultrasonic waves, the two are mixed quickly and evenly. The salt broth and chili oil are emulsified in less than a minute, and the entire soup is turned a uniform orange color.

Another advantage is that the emulsion made with an ultrasonic mixer is hard to decompose than the liquid mixed with a regular mixer. Ultra-

126　分子調理の日本食｜Molecular Cooking in Japanese Cuisine

sonic devices are often utilized in the food processing field for dispersion, emulsification, and the mixing of ingredients. For example, they are used in the production of mayonnaise and juice.

An emulsion is a mixture of liquids that separate each other, such as water and oil, but it is not just a simple mixture. One liquid forms tiny droplets, and they evenly disperse within the other liquid.

Emulsification has been applied for butter, margarine, salad dressing, and mayonnaise. The first two are the w/o (water in oil) type of emulsions that are water dispersed in oil, while the latter two are the o/w (oil in water) type of emulsions that are oil is dispersed in water (Figure 6). Natural emulsifiers such as lipids and lipoproteins in milk, the ingredients in butter, help distribute water in fats and oils.

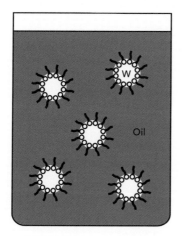

W/O type emulsion

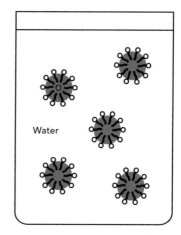

O/W type emulsion

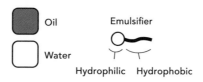

図6. エマルションのモデル図
Figure 6. Two typical types of emulsions

科学実験で使われている実験器具や実験機器には、調理に応用できる道具が数多く存在する。技能が高度に細分化されている道具たちは、調理の可能性を劇的に広げてくれる。新しい料理は、それまでの調理の世界にはなかった道具、手法、考えがもたらされたときに誕生する。

7

実験器具利用化

Utilization of laboratory equipment

There are a lot of laboratory equipment and instruments that can be applied to cooking. The skills are highly segmented, and they dramatically expand the possibilities of cooking. A whole new dish is often created when new tools, methods, and ideas are introduced in the culinary world.

分子調理の日本食 ｜ Molecular Cooking in Japanese Cuisine

超冷やし中華

Super-cold ramen

冷やし中華は暑くなり始める頃にメニューに登場する夏の定番料理だ。すさまじい猛暑を乗り越えるのに、"超" 冷やし中華はいかがだろうか。超低温の液体窒素で作ったスープとごま油の氷粒をかけて食べる、真夏の新メニューだ。

−196℃の液体窒素を使うと、液体スープは瞬時に凍って固体になる。急速にできた氷の結晶は、従来の冷凍技術で作ったものよりも粒子が細かい。うまく撹拌しながら作るとポロポロとした粒の塊になる。口の中で溶けていくときの舌触りは泡雪のようにとても繊細だ。

Hiyashi chuka (cold ramen) is a typical Japanese summer dish that appears on the menu during the hot season. How about trying "super" cold ramen to survive the extreme summer heat. This is a new noodle dish for mid-summer, with ice grains of soup and sesame oil made with ultra-low temperature liquid nitrogen, and are served on top of over the noodles.

Liquid nitrogen at −196℃ (−321℉) instantly freezes the liquid soup to a solid. These rapidly formed ice crystals are finer in particle size than those made by conventional freezing techniques. When the liquid is frozen with proper stirring, it turns into fine hailstones. The texture when they melt in the mouth is very delicate, like fragile snow crystals.

材料

- ・酢 … 75ml（大さじ5）
- ・しょうゆ … 60ml（大さじ4）
- ・砂糖 … 36g
- ・みりん … 30ml（大さじ2）
- ・水 … 30ml（大さじ2）
- ・ごま油 … 10ml（小さじ2）
- ・冷やし中華の麺と具材
  （きゅうり、ハム、錦糸たまご）

道具

- ・小鍋
- ・バット
- ・ガラスボウル
- ・泡だて器
- ・デュワー瓶
- ・スポイト
- ・液体窒素
- ・網しゃくし

手順

1. 中華タレをつくる。ごま油以外のタレの材料を小鍋に入れ、中火で沸騰直前まで温めたら火を止める。粗熱をとり、冷蔵庫でしっかり冷やす。

2. ゴーグルや手袋を装着し、液体窒素をデュワー瓶に用意する。

3. ガラスボウルに冷えた①を入れる。その上から液体窒素を数回に分けて注ぐ。

4. 泡だて器ですぐに攪拌し、そぼろ状になるまで液体窒素の追加と攪拌を繰り返す。

5. ゴマ油をスポイトにとり、液体窒素に滴下する。固まった粒を網しゃくしですくう。

6. 用意しておいた冷やし中華の具材の上に、④と⑤を振りかける。

INGREDIENTS

- · 75 ml (5 tablespoons) vinegar
- · 60 ml (4 tablespoons) soy sauce
- · 36 g sugar
- · 30 ml (2 tablespoons) mirin
- · 30 ml (2 tablespoons) water
- · 10 ml (2 teaspoons) sesame oil
- · hiyashi chuka noodles and toppings
  (cucumber, ham, and thinly
  shredded omelet)

UTENSILS

- · small pot
- · glass bowl
- · whisk
- · plastic pipette
- · skimmer
- · cooking tray
- · dewar vessel
- · liquid nitrogen

STEPS

1. Prepare the cold ramen soup. Put all the ingredients for the soup, except sesame oil, in a small pot. Heat it on medium until just before boiling, and turn off the heat. Place it in the refrigerator.

2. Put on goggles and gloves. Prepare liquid nitrogen in a dewar vessel.

3. Put the cold soup (#1) in a glass bowl. Pour liquid nitrogen into the bowl little by little.

4. Stir immediately with a whisk. Repeat adding liquid nitrogen and stirring to make coarse granules.

5. Suck up sesame oil with a plastic pipette and drip it into liquid nitrogen in the dewar vessel. Scoop the ice grains of sesame oil with a skimmer.

6. Serve the noodles and toppings on a plate and sprinkle #4 and #5 over them.

液体窒素を使って「冷却調理」をする
Use liquid nitrogen for "cooling cooking."

冷やし中華を食べると、最初は冷たくても、次第にぬるくなることにもどかしさを感じることはないだろうか。そんな時、冷やし中華のタレやごま油を液体窒素を使ってシャリシャリに凍らせ、上からかけておけば、冷たさを維持することができる。

液体窒素は、窒素を冷却して液体の状態にしたものだ。窒素は私たちが普段吸っている空気中に約78％含まれていることからわかるように、室温では気体で存在するが、−196℃より低い温度にすると液体になる。

調理に利用される低温の物質には、−79℃で昇華するドライアイス（冷凍した二酸化炭素）があるが、ドライアイスは固体なので使用できるものが限られる。一方、液体窒素は、食べ物や容器に注いで冷やすことができる。液体窒素の粘度は水の約5分の1であり、液体窒素は表面張力が比較的低いため、食品の粗い表面や不規則な表面の隅々に急速に流れ込み、食品全体を瞬時に凍らせる。液体窒素自体はすぐに気体となり、食品の中には留まらない。また、液体窒素は無色透明で無味無臭なため、食品の色や風味などに影響を及ぼさない。

人間が火を発見して以来、調理の中心は、食品を高温にさらし「熱を与える」ことであった。しかし、近年、液体窒素が「熱を奪う」新しい調理ツールとして、頻繁に使われるようになっている。

アイスクリームの場合、液体窒素で作ったものの方が従来の方法で作ったものよりも、氷の結晶が小さくなる。氷の結晶のサイズは、食べたときの冷たさや乳脂肪のクリーミーさの感覚を変化させることで、アイスクリームのおいしさに影響を与える。一般的に、凍結が速いほど、氷の結晶が小さくなり、食品の組織構造が壊れにくくなる。食感や香りを損なうことなく食品を凍結するには、凍結速度が重要である。

液体窒素を調理で使う際には、注意すべきことがある。液体窒素が皮膚に大量もしくは長時間触れた場合は凍傷になる。耐冷性のグローブや保護メガネなどを着け、充分安全に気をつけて使用することが大切である。また、液体窒素の保存や使用には、二重壁の内部を真空にした断熱容器のデュワー瓶などを用いる。液体窒素は−196℃で気化するときは、体積が約700倍になる。そのため、断熱容器は絶対に密閉してはいけない。液体窒素がたまっている容器を密閉すると、蒸発した窒素ガスが行き場を失い、容器が破損したり、最悪の場合、破裂したりする。また、室内で液体窒素を大量に使用した場合や、液体窒素の容器を長時間放置した場合、蒸発した窒素が空気を押しのけて、酸素濃度を下げる。その結果、特に密閉された小さな部屋や地下室などでは酸欠になる危険性がある。窒素は無色透明で無味無臭なため充満に気が付くのは困難であるため、換気を必ず行う必要がある。

Sometimes you may feel disappointed that hiyashi chuka lost its coldness while you are eating it. In that case, the ice granulated ramen soup or sesame oil made with liquid nitrogen can keep it cold.

Liquid nitrogen is nitrogen in a liquid state at low temperature. Nitrogen makes up 78% of the air and is gas in standard temperature and pressure. It becomes a liquid below −196°C (−321°F).

The well-known low-temperature substance used in cooking is dry ice (frozen carbon dioxide), which sublimates at −79°C (−110°F). However, dry ice is solid and is limited to its form for use. On the other hand, liquid nitrogen can be poured into foods or containers to cool them directly. The viscosity of liquid nitrogen is about one-fifth that of water, and the surface tension of liquid nitrogen is relatively low. It flows into every hole and corner of foods with rough or irregular surfaces and freezes them instantly. Liquid nitrogen itself quickly turns into a gas and leaves from the foods. Also, liquid nitrogen does not have any color, taste, and smell, so it does not affect foods' colors and flavors.

Even since human beings discovered fire, a significant part of cooking has been adding heat to the foods at high temperatures. However, in recent years, liquid nitrogen has been often used as a new cooking tool for "taking heat" from the foods.

The ice crystals of ice cream made with liquid nitrogen are smaller than those made by conventional methods. The ice crystals' size affects the deliciousness of the ice cream by altering the creamy texture of the milk fat and the coldness in the mouth. In general, fast freezing makes the ice crystals smaller, so the foods' tissue structure is hard to break down. Freezing speed is important in freezing foods without loss of texture and aroma.

There are a few precautions when using liquid nitrogen in cooking. Large-volume or long-term contact of liquid nitrogen with the skin causes frostbite. It is important to wear cold-resistant gloves and protective goggles and to use liquid nitrogen with great care for safety. Additionally, a dewar vessel, an insulated container with a vacuum inside the double-wall, is needed to store and use liquid nitrogen. Liquid nitrogen evaporates at −196°C and becomes about 700 times larger in volume. Therefore, the container with liquid nitrogen should never be sealed. If it were sealed, the evaporated nitrogen gas might break the container or, in the worst case, might rupture it. When a large amount of liquid nitrogen is used indoors or when the liquid nitrogen container is left for a long time, the evaporated nitrogen pushes the air away and lowers the oxygen concentration. As a result, there is a risk of oxygen depletion, especially in small and enclosed rooms or basements. Be sure to ventilate because it is hard to notice that nitrogen is filling the room, as the gas is colorless, tasteless, and scentless.

まさに "いちご大福"

Very true strawberry daifuku

この和菓子は、いちごを堪能するためにある。いちごの他に使う材料は少量の粉だけで、粉をこねる水分はいちごから取ってきたものだ。大福の皮もあんもいちごでできているから、和菓子というより、大福のようにモチモチとしたいちごを食べているようだ。

もしも、キッチンに遠心分離機があれば(!)、このシンプルでインパクトのある味が手軽に作れる。遠心分離は比重の違いで物質を分ける方法だ。いちごは上澄みと沈殿物とにきれいに分けられる。いちごの沈殿物は、そのまま使えば、種の食感が楽しいあんになる。

This is a soft rice cake for enjoying all the flavor of strawberries. The ingredients are just strawberries plus a small amount of rice flour. The liquid for kneading the dough as well as the paste stuffed into the rice cake are all gotten from strawberries. So it is like eating the strawberry, which has the sticky and chewy texture as daifuku, a Japanese confection.

Hypothetically, if you have a centrifuge in your kitchen (!), it becomes quite easy to make this simple and astonishing daifuku. Centrifugation is a method of separating substances according to the difference in specific gravity. The strawberries are clearly separated into the supernatant and the precipitate. The precipitate of strawberries can be used to make a paste with a pleasant texture of seeds.

材料

・いちご…4粒
・白玉粉…25g
・片栗粉…適量

道具

・耐熱ボウル
・菜箸
・木べら
・バット
・ブレンダー
・遠心チューブ
・遠心分離機
・電子レンジ

手 順

1. ヘタを取ったいちごをブレンダーで滑らかになるまで攪拌し、いちごソースを作る。

2. 遠心チューブに、いちごソースを入れる。

3. 5℃に冷却した遠心分離機で10,000G、30分の条件で遠心分離を行う。

4. いちごの上澄みの液体と沈殿物の固体にそれぞれ分ける。

5. 耐熱ボウルに白玉粉を入れ、いちごの上澄みを全量の1/3ほど加えてよく練る。残りも少しずつ加えながら、サラサラになるまでよく混ぜる。

6. 500Wの電子レンジで1分30秒間加熱し、湿らせた木べらで混ぜる。さらに1分間加熱し、艶が出るまで木べらでよく混ぜる。

7. 半透明になったら、片栗粉を敷いたバットの上に取り出し、全体に片栗粉をまぶす。

8. 粗熱をとってから必要な分をちぎり、丸めてから手で少しずつ押しつぶし、円盤状に形を整える。

9. ⑧の中央にいちご沈殿物を載せ、あふれないよう注意しながら口を閉じる。

1

3

4

INGREDIENTS

· 4 strawberries
· 25 g shiratamako (refined rice flour)
· potato starch, as needed

UTENSILS

· heat-resistant bowl
· cooking chopsticks
· wooden spatula
· cooking tray
· blender
· centrifuge tube
· centrifuge machine
· microwave oven

STEPS

1. Prepare the strawberry sauce. Hull the strawberries and mix them with a blender.

2. Put the strawberry sauce into a centrifuge tube.

3. Centrifuge at 5°C (41°F) and 10,000 G for 30 minutes.

4. Separate the strawberry's supernatant liquid and precipitate solid.

5. Put 1/3 of the strawberry supernatant and shiratamako in a heat-resistant bowl. Knead them well. Pour the rest of the supernatant little by little and mix well until the dough becomes smooth.

6. Heat the dough in a microwave oven at 500W for 1 minute 30 seconds and mix it with a wet wooden spatula. Heat again for 1 minute and mix well until the dough becomes glossy.

7. When the dough is translucent, transfer it to a cooking tray covered lightly with potato starch and coat it with the starch.

8. After the dough cools down, divide it into small pieces. Round them in the palm of your hand and then make a disk shape using the base of your thumb.

9. Place the strawberry precipitate in the center of the disk (#8). Wrap up the precipitate and pinch them closed.

6

7

9

解説
Explanation

ひとつの食材から
いくつもの新たな食材を生み出す
Many new ingredients can be created from a single ingredient.

　このいちご大福に使われている基本の材料は、いちごと白玉粉の2つだけである。砂糖も小豆のあんも、水すらも使っていない。まず、いちごをミキサーにかけたものを、遠心分離機を使って、上澄みの液体と沈殿物の固体に分ける。上澄みの液体を白玉粉に混ぜてもちを作り、沈殿物はそのままあんにする。遠心分離した上澄み液はいちごの赤い色が少し残っているため、もちは淡いピンク色になる。一方、あんはいちごそのものより濃い赤色をしており、味はより濃縮されている。食べたときの食感は大福だが、味や香りは甘酸っぱいいちごそのものだ。「まさにいちご」の大福である。

　レシピとは別に、いちごの他にも、りんご、ぶどう、スイカ、キウイフルーツなどさまざまな果物をつぶして遠心分離を行った。この操作により、比重の異なる成分に分けられるため、それぞれの成分を個別の食材として使うことが可能だ。遠心分離機に使う遠心管という容器に入れたまま凍らせて、ひとつの果物が何層にも分かれたアイスキャンディーを作ることもできる。トマトピューレやピーチネクターを上澄みの液体と沈殿物の固体に分けることで異なる食材を作り出し、それらの特徴を活かした新料理を開発することも実際に行われている。

　特に分けるとおもしろい食材は、鶏卵の黄身だろう。卵黄は、通常の遠心分離機よりも回転数を上げることができる超遠心分離器を使うと、上澄みの「プラズマ」と沈殿の「顆粒」という成分に分けることができる。この2つの成分の違いはすでに明らかになっていて、脂質とタンパク質に大きな差がある。プラズマ卵黄と顆粒卵黄をそれぞれフライパンで焼いて食べてみると、それぞれ風味は驚くほど違う。プラズマは脂質が多いせいか、やわらかいゴム状で、ちょうどプロセスチーズのような食感であり、それに対して顆粒は、粉っぽくパサパサしており、香りもやや弱い。プラズマと顆粒、それぞれに分けた卵黄を使ったオムレツなどは、通常の卵黄を使ったものと味や香り、食感などがかなり異なるだろう。

The only two basic ingredients used for this strawberry daifuku are strawberry and shiratamako. Typical ingredients of usual daifuku, sugar, red bean paste, and even water, are not used. First, strawberries are mashed with a blender and are separated into the supernatant liquid and the precipitate solid by a centrifugal machine. The supernatant liquid is mixed with shiratamako to make the dough, and the precipitated solid is wrapped into the dough as a filling. The dough is a pink tint because the supernatant liquid retains the red color of strawberry slightly. On the other hand, the filling is a darker red color than the original strawberry, and its taste is also concentrated. The texture is the same as a traditional daifuku, but its flavor is sweet and sour strawberry. This is the strawberry daifuku. Very true.

Outside this recipe, various fruits such as apples, grapes, watermelons, and kiwifruits were centrifuged. Since they are divided into components with different specific gravities, each component can be used as an individual food ingredient. Freezing the centrifuge tubes containing the centrifugal products can be made a multi-layered popsicle. Distinct ingredients are produced by dividing tomato puree and peach nectar into supernatant liquid and precipitate solids, and new dishes that take advantage of these characteristics are already created.

A chicken egg yolk is a particularly interesting ingredient to divide. Using an ultracentrifuge with higher speeds than an ordinary centrifuge, the yolk is separated the components into the supernatant "plasma" and the precipitate "granules." The significant differences in lipids and proteins between the two components have been proven. Pan-fried plasma and granules egg yolks have a surprisingly different flavor. The plasma egg yolk is a soft, rubbery, and a processed cheese-like texture, while the granule egg yolk is a dry and powdery texture with a slightly weaker aroma. Using separated yolks, plasma, and granules could create an omelet that is quite different in flavor and texture from one with the regular yolk.

おでんですよ！　肉じゃがですよ！　すき焼きですよ！

Tasty leftover's sauce

炊きたてのご飯にのせて食べる海苔の佃煮は、海のおいしさがつまった味がする。一方、こちらは、おでんや肉じゃが、すき焼きのおいしさを文字どおり凝縮させた料理である。

ロータリーエバポレーターという機械を使って、おでんや肉じゃが、すき焼きの煮汁を濃縮した。この装置は、減圧状態を作り出すことで溶液の沸点を下げ、溶液の濃縮をしやすくする。煮汁も焦がすことなく水分を飛ばすことが可能だ。科学の実験室では古くから使われている不思議な形状の機械だが、分野を超えて、分子調理のキッチンにも設置されるようになった。

Nori-no-tsukudani (laver boiled in soy sauce), eaten with freshly cooked rice, is full of the sea's deliciousness. On the other hand, the dishes in our recipe are the delicious concentrates of Japanese simmered dishes: oden, nikujaga, and sukiyaki.

A rotary evaporator machine is used to concentrate the cooking liquids of oden, nikujaga, and sukiyaki. The device depressurizes the inside of the flask, thereby lowering the solution's boiling point and facilitating the solution's concentration. The water in the cooking liquids can be removed without burning it. This curiously shaped machine has been used for a long time in science laboratories since long ago, but it is also placed in molecular cooking kitchens beyond fields these days.

・おでんの煮汁
・肉じゃがの煮汁
・すき焼きの煮汁

・ロータリーエバポレーター
・なす型フラスコ

1. エバポレーター内の冷却水を循環させ、ウォータバスを40℃に設定する。

2. おでんや肉じゃが、すき焼きの煮汁をそれぞれなす型フラスコに注ぐ。

3. フラスコをロータリーエバポレーターに取り付ける。真空ポンプでフラスコ内を減圧し、フラスコを回転させながら煮汁を濃縮する。

4. 1時間ほど減圧濃縮した後、濃縮物を回収する。

INGREDIENTS

· leftover soup of oden
    (dish of various ingredients, e.g.
    boiled egg, daikon, processed
    fishcakes, etc. stewed in a light
    soy-flavored dashi broth)
· leftover soup of nikujaga
    (dish of meat, potatoes, and
    onion stewed in sweetened soy
    sauce and mirin)
· leftover soup of sukiyaki
    (dish of meat, vegetables, and
    other ingredients simmered
    in a mixture of soy sauce,
    sugar, and mirin)

UTENSILS

· rotary evaporator
· recovery flask

STEPS

1. Circulate the cooling water in the rotary evaporator and set the water bath to 40℃ (104°F).

2. Pour leftover soup of oden, nikujaga, and sukiyaki into a recovery flask separately.

3. Attach the flask to the evaporator. Start evaporating. The inside of the flask is depressurized with a vacuum pump and the leftover soup is concentrated while rotating the flask.

4. After concentrating under reduced pressure for about 1 hour, collect the concentrate.

2

2

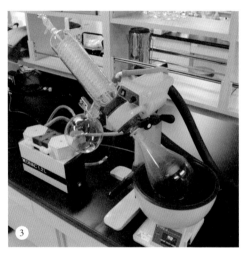

3

3

4

新しい料理は、新しい道具から
New dishes come from new tools.

　おでん、肉じゃが、すき焼きなどの具材はおいしいが、その煮汁もまたおいしい。煮汁には調味料だけでなく、それぞれの具材からのうまみが染み出て、足し算されているからだ。おいしさのつまった煮汁をメインとして堪能できる料理が作れないかと考えた。

　ロータリーエバポレーターを使って煮汁を濃縮すると、短時間のうちに水分だけが蒸発する。できあがったおでん、肉じゃが、すき焼きの煮汁の濃縮物は、どろっとした糊状の物質だ。ひとなめするだけで"脳に突き刺さる"くらいのうま味があるペーストである。温かいごはんの上にかければいくらでも箸が進む。

　煮汁を火にかけて煮詰め続けると焦げてしまう。糖とタンパク質が反応するメイラード反応が起こることが原因だ。焦がさずに、煮汁からおいしい成分を取り出すには、水分だけをうまく蒸発させることがポイントである。それを行えるのが、液体を減圧下で蒸発・濃縮させるロータリーエバポレーターである。溶液を入れた容器内を減圧させることで、溶媒の沸点が下がり、比較的低温でも液体が除去されるため、果物から香り高いフレーバーを濃縮することなどにも使われている。

　これまでにも先駆的なシェフたちは、実験室レベルの器具を調理器具として用い、料理の可能性を広げてきた。科学実験で古くから使われている実験器具や実験機器は、その原理を考えると、料理に応用できる宝の山のように思えてくる。

　特に分離、濃縮、乾燥、撹拌、精製、温度調節に関する機器類は、高度に細分化されている。たとえば、ある食材を乾燥させて粉にしたいとき、冷却と加熱がコントロールできる「凍結乾燥機」を使えば、食材の風味を最大限に活かした状態での粉末化が可能である。さらにその粉末をさまざまなメッシュでできた「ふるい振とう機」を使ってマイクロメートル単位の粒形に分ければ、舌ざわりの異なる粉末をいくつも得ることができる。また、物質を細かく粉砕し、均一化する「ホモジナイザー」は、やわらかい動物の臓器を超音波を使って均一にするものや、硬い歯や骨を分銅によって粉々にするものなど、各種取りそろえられている。これらを使えば、通常混ざらないような食材同士も均一に混ぜ合わせることが可能だ。

　人間が道具を使って調理するようになってから、料理は進化してきた。調理の長い系譜の中で、分子調理の分野でも、さまざまな調理道具が誕生し、料理もまた進化していくことだろう。

The ingredients for oden, nikujaga, and sukiyaki are delicious, but the leftover cooking liquid is also excellent because the umami from the ingredients and the seasonings seeps into the water and is combined. This recipe is inspired by a desire to make such a delicious leftover into the main dish.

When a rotary evaporator is used to concentrate the leftover soup, the water evaporates quickly. The concentrate of leftover soup from oden, nikujaga, and sukiyaki is a thick, viscous paste-like substance. A lick of this paste activates the appetite. Hot rice with the paste on top can be eaten forever.

Continuing to boil the leftover soup, it will burn. This is because of the Maillard reaction, in which sugar and protein react with each other. A rotary evaporator, which evaporates and concentrates the liquid under reduced pressure, can solve this problem. The solution's boiling point is lowered by reducing the pressure, and only water can be removed at a relatively low temperature. Therefore, it is also utilized for concentrating the concentration of fragrant flavors from fruits.

Pioneering chefs have used laboratory-level equipment as cooking utensils to expand the possibilities of cooking. The laboratory equipment and apparatus that have been used in scientific experiments over the centuries seem to be a treasure trove of culinary applications.

The equipment for separation, concentration, drying, agitation, purification, and temperature control is highly subdivided. For example, a "freeze dryer" dries and powderizes the ingredients keeping the flavors by controlling the cooling and heating. Besides, a "sieve shaker" divides the powder into micrometer-sized particles with various types of meshes, resulting in a variety of powders with different textures. A homogenizer has many functions, such as homogenizing soft animal organs with ultrasonic waves or shattering hard teeth and bones with weights. The homogenizer can mix ingredients that would typically not mix.

Cooking has evolved since humans began to cook with tools. In the long lineage of cooking, a variety of cooking tools have been created in molecular cooking, and the evolution of the dishes will keep going.

おわりに

　この本を作るにあたり、著者らは約一年間、ディスカッションや試作に明け暮れてきました。「分子調理法」×「日本食（≒馴染み深い料理）」というテーマで料理を考えながら、料理の形になっていないものも数多く作りました。その過程を終えて心に強く残っているのは、共にじっくりものを創り上げていく中で、思いもよらない結果がたくさん生まれたということです。それは同時に、興奮と面白さを感じる時間でもありました。同じ食材、同じメニューであっても、人によってその捉え方は違います。異なる視点が増えることで、いろいろな気づきがあり、さらに新しい発想が生まれることもあります。この本に載っている料理がなんとか形になったのは、著者らの考え方の違いを突き合わせ、時間をかけて検討したからです。

　現在、分子調理法は、特定の人が特定の場所で特別の料理に用いる傾向があります。けれども、私達には、身近な手段としての分子調理の可能性を示したいという共通の想いがありました。新たな調理法は、料理の世界に選択肢を増やし、その世界をより豊かにしてくれます。

　今回作った料理は、著者らの空想の料理を実験室で現実化したものです。皆さんも、頭の中で空想の料理を創ったり、食べたい料理を想像して実際に作ったりした経験があるのではないでしょうか。頭の中に思い描く料理には、現実に存在するものよりも、遥かにたくさんの斬新な料理があります。自分の空想を叶える調理法のひとつとして、私たちは分子調理法をキッチンに迎え入れる日が来るかもしれません。

　日々の生活において変わるもの、変わらないもの、残るもの、残らないものは数多くあります。もちろん料理も同様です。私達それぞれが今日まで食べてきたものは、料理の歴史の一部でもあります。これから先の料理は未知の歴史です。この本で紹介したメニューや、それぞれが日々食べる料理、さらに頭の中の空想料理は、どのように進化していくのでしょうか。さまざまな視点を持ちながら、まだ誰も出会ったことのない料理を皆さんと生み出していければと思います。

　本の制作で、たくさんの方にお世話になりました。深く感謝申し上げます。編集者の田村英男さん、デザイナーの中西要介さん、写真家のyoshimiさん、翻訳に関わっていただいた稲垣陽子さんと川端デイビッドさん、この本を作るきっかけをくださった水原文さん、本当にありがとうございました。

著者一同

分子調理の日本食 ｜ Molecular Cooking in Japanese Cuisine

Conclusion

We had immersed in discussing and experimenting with making the recipes throughout the year. We started with the idea of applying the "molecular cooking technology" to ordinary Japanese cuisine, and sometimes, we made something that did not look like foods. What most impressed us was that unexpected, amazing results were produced by spending a lot of time together to create things. It was a very exciting and interesting time. We all have our own perspectives and attitudes on the same foods or the same dishes. It reminded us that these could lead to diverse insights and new ideas. This book is the result of taking the time to study the differences between us.

On the other hand, we had a common wish. Although the molecular cooking technology currently tends to be used by certain people in certain places for special, mainly expensive, dishes, we wanted to find the potential of the technology for familiar uses. The new cooking method is sure to add one more option to everyday cooking and enrich that world.

All the dishes in this book were made in the laboratory. Although they are now at the laboratory-level, the day would come when you welcome the molecular cooking techniques into your home kitchens as one of the daily cooking methods. You may have imagined dishes you wanted to eat and then actually cooked these or created your own fictional dishes. There are far more innovative dishes that you can imagine in your head than exist in reality. One day, you may be able to eat any dishes that you have made in your imagination.

Like many things, some foods and dishes change and others do not change during our lives. The dishes in this book, the dishes we eat every day, and the dishes in our imaginations also evolve. What you have cooked or eaten until today is a part of the history of cooking. What you cook or eat tomorrow is the future history of cooking. We hope to be able to create the "history" that no one has ever cooked before. We hope you will be there too.

We appreciate all the support in creating this book. We want to thank Hideo Tamura for editing, Yosuke Nakanishi for book design, yoshimi for photography, Yoko Inagaki and David Kawabata for helping in translation, and Bun Mizuhara for allowing us to make this book. Thank you.

The authors

索引　　　　　　　　　INDEX

写真撮影

yoshimi
カバー, 003, 008, 010, 016, 022, 029, 030, 036, 042,
048, 050, 056, 062, 068, 070, 076, 082, 088, 090, 096,
102, 108, 110, 116, 122, 128, 130, 136, 142, 148, 150

石川繭子
012, 013, 018, 019, 024, 025, 032, 033, 038, 039, 044,
045, 053, 058, 059, 065, 073, 078, 079, 084, 085, 093,
098, 099, 105, 113, 118, 119, 125, 133, 138, 139, 145

Photo Credit

yoshimi
cover, 003, 008, 010, 016, 022, 029, 030, 036, 042,
048, 050, 056, 062, 068, 070, 076, 082, 088, 090, 096,
102, 108, 110, 116, 122, 128, 130, 136, 142, 148, 150

ISHIKAWA Mayuko
012, 013, 018, 019, 024, 025, 032, 033, 038, 039, 044,
045, 053, 058, 059, 065, 073, 078, 079, 084, 085, 093,
098, 099, 105, 113, 118, 119, 125, 133, 138, 139, 145

Art Direction
NAKANISHI Yosuke (STUDIO PT.)

Book Design
NAKANISHI Yosuke, NEZU Koharu (STUDIO PT.)

著者紹介

石川 伸一（いしかわ しんいち）

分子調理学者。宮城大学食産業学群教授。分子調理研究会（www.molcookingsoc.org）
代表。食を「アート×サイエンス×デザイン×エンジニアリング」とクロスさせて研究している
（www.ishikawalab.com）。

石川 繭子（いしかわ まゆこ）

イラスト作成・執筆などをおこなっている。「ひとさじのかがく舎（www.1tspscience.com）」
で食と科学についての活動に取り組む。食に関する生物学、哲学、文化人類学に興味が
ある。

桑原 明（くわばら あかり）

宮城大学食産業学部卒業。同大学院博士前期課程に入学。魔法のような食を作るため
に、分子調理法を用いた新しい料理・調理に関心を持つ。

About the authors

ISHIKAWA Shin-ichi

Molecular cooking scientist. Professor, at School of Food Industrial Sciences, Miyagi
University. Representative for the Molecular Cooking Society (www.molcookingsoc.
org). My research crosses food with "art × science × design × engineering."

ISHIKAWA Mayuko

Illustrator and writer. Working in a group "1 tsp science" (www.1tspscience.com) on food
and science. Interested in the biology, philosophy, and cultural anthropology of food.

KUWABARA Akari

Graduated from the School of Food Industrial Sciences, Miyagi University. Entered
the Master's Course in the Graduate School of Food, Agricultural and Environmental
Sciences at the same university. Interested in new dishes and cooking using molecular
cooking methods to create magical foods.

分子調理の日本食

2021年 4月23日 初版第1刷発行

著者	石川 伸一 (いしかわ しんいち)、
	石川 繭子 (いしかわ まゆこ)、
	桑原 明 (くわばら あかり)
発行人	ティム・オライリー
アートディレクション	
	中西要介 (STUDIO PT.)
デザイン	中西要介、根津小春 (STUDIO PT.)
印刷・製本	日経印刷株式会社
発行所	株式会社オライリー・ジャパン
	〒160-0002 東京都新宿区四谷坂町12番22号
	Tel (03) 3356-5227 Fax (03) 3356-5263
	電子メール japan@oreilly.co.jp
発売元	株式会社オーム社
	〒101-8460 東京都千代田区神田錦町3-1
	Tel (03) 3233-0641 (代表) Fax (03) 3233-3440

Printed in Japan (ISBN978-4-87311-948-9)